MYTH, IMMORALITY, AND AMERICAN IMPERIALISM

★★★ AND ★★★

HENRY F. ZACCHINI

2008 by Henry Zacchini

Book design: Andy West

ISBN: 978-1-60571-013-6
Library of Congress Control Number: 2008907366

Printed in the United States of America

For Rachel

"But it was impossible to save the Great Republic. She was rotten to the heart. Lust of conquest had long ago done its work; trampling upon the helpless abroad had taught her, by a natural process, to endure with apathy the like at home; multitudes who had applauded the crushing of other people's liberties, lived to suffer for their mistake in their own persons. The government was irrevocably in the hands of the prodigiously rich and their hangers-on; the suffrage was become a mere machine, which they used as they chose. There was no principle but commercialism, no patriotism but of the pocket."

– MARK TWAIN

CONTENTS

ACKNOWLEDGMENTS

Many people helped in the production of this book and I owe a debt of gratitude to all of them. Any of the work's qualities can be attributed to the able assistance I received and any of its shortcomings are strictly my own.

A hearty thank you to my editors, all of whom made this book readable: Nate Nickerson, Alyssa Grossman, Jennifer Stapper, Rachel Glickman, Andy Smith-Petersen, Sharon Matzek and Greg Joly. I would also like to thank Laura Dove, Bo Sherman, Laura Patterson, Rachel Glickman, Andy West and Andy Smith-Petersen for their help in choosing a design for the book. A special thank you to Andy West who did all of the wonderful design and layout work on the book; it is a joy to look at on account of his efforts. I also want to extend a sincere thank you to Lucy and the staff at Northshire Press who are a godsend for unknown Vermont writers.

Lastly, a big thank you to all of my friends and family who did not work directly on the book, but whose love, understanding and humor have made me who I am and have given me the courage, compassion and strength to critically assess the problems we face in the world.

INTRODUCTION

I began writing this book in 1999. At that time, mainstream renderings of American imperialism were largely unspoken and unseen. The public at large appeared to accept the United States' militarism as part of our historic role as humble world police officers; making the world safe for our vision of unitary, capitalistic oligarchy. Even seemingly blatant excesses like the constant bombing of Iraqi and Serbian civilians could not wake the country from its communal stupor.

But something strange happened following the election of the second Mr. Bush and his rabble. Old ideas surrounding the United States' benign foreign interventions and entanglements started to fall by the wayside in the harsh light of Bush's version of American fascism. It was as if the United States were transported from a being a hapless cop into a ruthless criminal overnight. The same intelligentsia who were willing to turn a blind eye to the Clintonian immoderation that occurred in the 1990's were now deeply alarmed by the United States' internal and external behavior. And this sudden alarm was reflected in the titles on bookshelves and in much of the "liberal" media. How was it possible, they would ask, for a country to fall so fast and so far in such a brief amount of time?

Americans are above all politically hopeful, which is to say, politically naïve, ever expecting that a person or party will save us from our government's misdeeds and put us back on our pre-destined, righteous path. Indeed, the people's struggle for freedom and democracy against fascism and imperialism has been the overarching narrative of this country. But, America's past is written in the blood of the oppressed, and its imperial aspirations were present from the moment Europeans set their feet on the soil of this land. Once we accept that reality, we can squarely look at what is happening in contemporary America as part of a larger picture and not as an aberrant event. If you are willing to dig deeper into our collective mythology, read on, and perhaps together we can catch a glimpse of what lies behind the wall of fantasy.

1

THE MYTH OF DEMOCRACY

"The proposition that the people are the best keepers of their own liberties is not true. They are the worst conceivable, they are no keepers at all; they can neither judge, act, think, or will as a political body."

– JOHN ADAMS

"Civil government, so far as it is instituted for the security of property, is in reality instituted for the defense of the rich against the poor, or of those who have some property against those who have none at all."

– ADAM SMITH

Youth who undergo an American public education are instructed from a very young age that the founding principle of the United States is democracy. The word democracy appears repeatedly from the inception of the American child's education. Democracy carries massive weight as a propaganda tool because it has tremendously positive connotations. It is one of a select group of words, such as "love," "peace" and "freedom," that have few detractors. Somewhat tragically, the dominant political culture in the United States is so far removed from democracy, that although the word is continually employed, it has become largely meaningless.

A representative democracy is a government directly elected by majority vote, that recognizes and honors the civil liberties and human rights of its citizens, and acknowledges that the authority to govern is not pre-ordained but a privilege granted by the people. There are many at home and abroad who would contend, given this definition, that the United States is indeed a democratic country. In order to lay open the myth of democracy and understand why the present government behaves undemocratically, there are a number of important variables to consider.

To determine the historical factors that may have conspired against democracy, it is essential to focus on the origins of American society from the earliest colonial settlements through George Washington's presidency. During this period, the drama of individuals struggling against tyranny and the eventual triumph of power over democracy poignantly unfolds. Conflicts between power and democracy are inchoate to the foundation of American society. They also help explain governmental developments consistent with imperial power but inconsistent with democracy. Imperial power holds nothing less than antipathy for democratic principles, as its very existence is predicated on democracy's absence. The following historical exploration is not intended to be a comprehensive analysis of colonial America; rather, it is focused on the manifestations of democracy and authority in the 17th and 18th centuries.

ELITISM AND THEOCRACY

It is well documented that the American colonies began as a place of refuge for some Europeans, a place to make a fortune for others, and a place of enslavement for indentured servants and Africans. When historical anecdotes about these early non-native people are retold, the descriptions often simplify their lives. There are stories regaling the Puritans' escape from religious persecution in England or of the initial suffering and eventual prosperity of the New York, Massachusetts Bay and Virginia colonies. Governance in early America is sometimes neglected in the retelling of these tales, but it was governance that connected the lives of the original colonists, bound the various members of these communities together and created a shared experience which crossed religious, class and racial lines.

Members of the elite clergy and gentry viewed America as an environment where they could exert their authority over others. For religious and financial purposes, the male leaders of the original colonies were able to exercise substantial control over their subjects (Hockett 1931, p. 29; Johnson 1997, p.39). The original settlements were fairly easy to control; they were small, insular communities beset by tremendous difficulties ranging from potential starvation to attacks from Native Americans. To retain order, the colonial leaders would cite English law in administering authority, and then enact their own form of justice (or dismiss judges) when the prevailing English laws were deemed too lenient or inapplicable (Bailyn & Fleming 1967, p. 53; Strout 1963, p. 5). The legions of slaves, indentured servants, and laborers who comprised the majority of the population (and who were relied upon to drive the engine of the early colonial economy), were afforded little to no chance of enjoying civil liberties or of electing their rulers, and did not experience any real sense of freedom.

In Massachusetts, the incipient political development was theocratic in nature. By 1660, more than a generation after the colony was established, only twenty percent of the white male population, sanctioned by the church, was eligible to vote (Granville 1925, p. 44). The theocracy, which inspired rampant religious intolerance, was not isolated to Massachusetts, but widespread throughout the settlements. America was, in general, a land of persecution for individuals who fell out of line with a community's religious beliefs. While the typical education for the contemporary American child preaches that many people came to the United States to escape religious persecution, the opposite can be convincingly argued. The extreme level of religious intolerance which defined the early colonial period is seldom acknowledged (other than a passing reference to the Salem Witch Trials-portrayed as an anomaly) (Beard 1968, p. 34; Granville 1925, p. 45-46; Hofstadter and Wallace 1970, p. 295; Mason 1956, p. 53). Although many of Massachusetts' initial colonists did come to America in order to escape persecution; it was their subsequent intolerance of others, and not their escape from British persecution, which set the tenor of America's legacy of prejudice.

Most white colonists came to America to work for European companies or the Crown, not to escape persecution. Settlements funded by companies or the Crown were under contract to pay back the price of their voyage with the riches they extracted from the New World. Even the religious zealots on the Mayflower shared their ship with non-Puritan individuals who were sent along by the London businessmen who financed the Mayflower's passage. These romanticized tales of persecution have proven more mythically appealing than stories about people trying to make money. The use of the Puritans as the symbol of early American history is therefore iconographically logical. Nonetheless, fortune seekers and the gentry played an equally important role in the formation of American society. And given the state of affairs in modern America, their legacy of avarice, much like the aforementioned religious intolerance, left a far more lasting impression on this country than the Puritans' moral austerity.

Because the colonial governors were ostensibly granted dictatorial powers to run their governments (insofar as they remained obsequious to the king, the church, or their company), they had tremendous latitude in determining their jurisdiction's political culture. Had they placed great importance on voting and the civil rights of their constituents, colonial life would certainly have reflected those beliefs. It would be nearly impossible to comprehensively gauge the perspectives of the dozens of pre-Revolutionary colonial governors with regards to democracy. However, a quick stock of their attitudes towards the masses points to the notion that it was their intransigence (in the face of mounting resistance to their policies) that partially contributed to the eventual onset of the American Revolution.

John Winthrop, the first governor of the Massachusetts Bay colony, believed democracy to be the worst form of government (Caldwell 1925, p.45) and exemplified the colonial governors' mentality. Winthrop came from a wealthy British family and shared the aristocracy's standard view of the rabble. His perception of liberty for the people was paternalistic, with authorities like himself, acting as benevolent, ordained rulers:

*If you stand for your natural corrupt liberties, and will do what is good in your
own eyes, you will not endure the least weight of authority, but will murmur,
and oppose, and be always striving to shake off that yoke; but if you will be satisfied to enjoy such civil and lawful liberties, such as Christ allows you, then
will you quietly and cheerfully submit unto that authority which is set over
you, in all the administrations of it, for your good (Mason 1956, p. 62).*

The invocation of Christ as his legislative partner is not remarkable considering Massachusetts' 17th century theocratic culture. What it heralds are similar
manifestations of bourgeois ideology in the post-revolutionary leaders' concept
of proper governance and attitude towards the disenfranchised. His statement
foreshadowed the dominant belief espoused by the "founding fathers," that true
democracy was a threat to liberty and that the ruling class has an obligation, as
the most enlightened (and most propertied) members of society, to exert their
authority for the good of society.

While religious intolerance continued throughout the 18th century
(Middlekauff 1982, p.43), and the majority of colonial leaders (governors
and their appointees) continued to come from the elite classes (Higham
1980, p. 61-62), another element began to emerge in the colonial governmental structure. The colonial assemblies were the colonies' version of
America's present day House of Representatives. It was through these bodies
that the class of well-off farmers, merchants, artisans, etc. were able to participate and thus partially mold government to their own image and need.
Contemporary estimates put colonial white male suffrage during this period
between 50 and 75 percent depending on local governmental regulations.
Although it varied from colony to colony, individuals granted voting privileges generally had to prove they possessed a prescribed amount of property
or land. By the time of the Revolution, the participation of these "freeholders" in the governmental process was widespread and accompanied by tangible power. And while their participation does not provide evidence of a pre-
Revolutionary democracy, it did play a role in fomenting the Revolution.
This manifestation of limited suffrage was one factor which led to the adop-

tion of the decentralized, state-centered, somewhat democratic Articles of Confederation as the initial U.S. governmental system.

SLAVERY, OPPRESSION AND GENOCIDE

Slavery was not an invention of the American colonists; it had been a common human economic implement for centuries. The essential rationale behind empires encouraging slave-based economies lay in their formidable social control structures, as slave labor satisfied the state's pressing needs for inexpensive labor and maximum production.

The first century of American colonization was marked by a preponderance of servitude, especially in the southern colonies. It has been estimated that in 17th century Virginia, seventy five percent of the population were servants of some kind (Takaki 1993, p. 54). Not all blacks who lived in the colonies during the 17th century were slaves and not all servants were black, as there were also thousands of white indentured servants (from all over Great Britain) in 17th century America. Gradually, throughout the 1600's a distinct class of white plantation owners began to emerge in the southern colonies. These individuals were (or, less commonly, became) members of the elite and were the product of a growing demand in the mother country for raw materials such as rice and tobacco. As the planter class cultivated their power, they began to make laws institutionalizing their most cost-effective form of labor, African slavery. In the 1660's, Virginia and Maryland passed laws that legitimized slavery, distinguished black labor from white labor, and dictated that a person born into slavery would remain a slave for life (Jones 1983, p. 22).

America's slave system was closely tied to the British Empire's colonialism, the basic tenets of which were to convert "savages," to develop markets for goods, and to acquire cheap raw materials. British colonization was built upon a system holding the mother country as the authority and the colonies as her subjects. Slavery, in addition to being the preferred labor of the planter class, was part of a methodical program of the mother country, whose policies were profoundly racist, rooted fundamentally in a philosophy of dominance and submission. The endemic racism of the white Europeans does not fully explain the outrages perpetrated against the slaves. Economic variables and the expansion of the previously referenced control structures also played a vital role in America's rapidly expanding slave labor system. The turn of the century marked the southern economies' transition from local agrarianism to one fully dependent on slave labor. By the 18th century, all of the southern states had large, powerful plantation owners, who organized a political and security structure which protected the planters' interests. These included a deregulated slave trade and legal systems that acted as a guardian for, and promoter of lawful slavery. The total number of African slaves in the colonies grew from an estimated 20,000 in 1700 to 350,000 by 1763 (Jones 1983, p. 22). In 1790, almost 15 years after the Declaration of Independence (and following the ratification of the Constitution), there were more than 650,000 slaves in the south, representing 33.5% percent of that region's population (Kolchin 1987, p. 53). It would take decades and the bloodiest war in American history before African Americans were manumitted, and more than 170 years from the Constitution's ratification before they were granted equal treatment under the law. These facts alone dispel much of the myth surrounding America's democratic inheritance.

Native Americans, like most African-Americans, were forcibly removed from their homeland and enslaved by the Europeans. However, due to their strong social fabric, knowledge of the terrain, high death rates from newly introduced diseases and military organization, their enslavement never matched the level of African enslavement. Their gradual eradication, beginning with the first permanent European communities, would eventually reach genocidal proportions.

Without belaboring the point, it would be irresponsible to not briefly reference the attitudes of the white population towards Native Americans in the colonial era. While there were atrocities committed by both sides in the conflicts that arose between Native Americans and the white colonists, the Europeans' actions towards the indigenous peoples were based in a belief that the American

Indians were savages. After a particularly brutal white raid on a Pequot village in 1636, Cotton Mather, a contemporary theologian, wrote that , "...no less than 600 Pequot souls were brought down to hell that day." (Zinn 1995, p. 15) Attitudes such as this helped to justify the non-natives' genocidal actions and their disregard for the humanity of indigenous people.

Denigration remains one of the most effective tools for dehumanizing a given body of individuals. As we have seen, Native Americans and blacks were both seen by Europeans as "savage" or less than human, paving the way for and mitigating any nefarious action against them. Anti-Native Americanism was particularly intense in the early days of New England's religious fanaticism when church leaders ecumenically portrayed Native Americans as devils (Takaki 1993, p. 40-41). The stereotype was not without consequences; along with attempts at Christian conversion, the Native American population in New England was decimated by European diseases and military attacks, with their numbers declining by an estimated 60,000 between 1610 and 1675 (Takaki 1993, p. 39). Similar results unfolded throughout the colonies as white settlers looked to expand their holdings deeper into the North American wilderness. In Virginia (as in New England), significant Native American populations were almost non-existent by the middle of the 17th century (Jones 1983, p. 32). Tribes in the Carolinas and New York also suffered great losses at the hands of the non-natives during the colonial period (Jones 1983, p. 32).

Black, Native American and white women experienced a similarly harsh reality in colonial America. Seen as chattel, whose primary function was to serve the needs of their families and husbands, they were afforded few privileges and even fewer civil rights. It would take, as was the case for African-Americans and Native Americans, generations for women to gain the rights of suffrage and equal protection under the law; rights considered fundamental to modern perceptions of what constitutes a representative democracy.

In recent years there has been a strong backlash against historians who argue that the limited scope of early American democracy is proven by the powerlessness of blacks, women, indentured servants, the indigent and Native Americans. They claim that one cannot apply 20th century standards of democracy to an 18th century society. The beautiful folly of this argument is neither can one claim, by today's definition, that early America was actually a democracy. One may even argue that, by contemporary criteria, not only was early America a democracy of limited scope; it was not really a democracy at all. The myth as it is ordinarily presented, simply states that America was born of democratic principles and is never accompanied by a qualifier, such as "...democratic principles consistent with 18th century notions of democracy." Thus one is led to believe that representative democracy as we understand it today is no different from its 18th century American manifestation. This logic unwittingly demands that the disenfranchised be considered within the context of America's nascent "democracy."

Considering all of the foregoing evidence, it is not difficult to understand the undemocratic outcome of the American Revolution. Although the leaders of the Revolution attempted to galvanize public opinion in support of their cause with calls of democracy and freedom (i.e. Jefferson's Declaration of Independence), the political culture that evolved from the war never achieved its professed ideals. These early leaders, like modern day mythmakers, knew the power of their words, but lived in a world insulated from their meaning. This explains, in part, why Jefferson's declaration is so often invoked by dissenting Americans: it espouses an archetype which has never been approached, and is a constant reminder of the Revolution's democratic failure.

REVOLUTIONARY FERVOR?

As mentioned earlier, both the growing power of the colonial assemblies, led by propertied men, and the governors' stubbornness in the face of this constituency's mounting opposition to Imperial policies, helped spark the revolution. In reality however, the governors' policies by the time of the Revolution had not changed much from those earlier in the 18th century. What had changed was the attitude of the mother country towards the enforcement of unpopular laws.

By 1763, following the English victory in the French and Indian War, the British government found itself in a ruinous financial situation. The country, partly as a result of the war with the French, languished in a depression. Depression in the mother country placed the heavily dependent American colonies in similarly poor financial straits. England believed that tighter enforcement of colonial taxation laws was a viable solution to its cash flow problems. This solution, in light of the British army having neutralized the French threat to the colonists (and given the Empire's perspective of the colonies as subservient to its wishes), seemed logical to the British government. Thus the mother country began demanding that the colonial governors more strictly levy tax laws, by military force if necessary, onto an already depressed American economy.

Partially in reaction to these newly enforced laws, the class of individuals most affected by the changes became vocal dissenters. The leaders of this opposition were politically astute men, who understood that gathering popular support for a revolution was much easier when the reasons for the revolt were "democracy" and "freedom" as opposed to money or control of markets.[i] In the years after the French and Indian War, the political situation for the colonists differed insignificantly from previous periods of colonial history, as the colonial assemblies retained their power, and the majority accepted their status as subjects of the British Crown. The cyclical downturn in the colonial economy and stiffer tax enforcement by the mother country were not alone sufficient expedients for the Revolution. The crucial change was the perspective of some members of the moneyed colonial class to their master.

Even with the powerful words of men such as Jefferson, Benjamin Franklin and Thomas Paine ringing in their ears, the support among white colonists for the Revolution was hardly fervent. Some estimates surmise that a potential majority of whites remained indifferent to the Revolutionary cause or were pro-British (Carroll & Noble 1977, p.116). Lack of support for the war may be explained by the relative difficulty of conveying news over great distances, or by the fact that many people (perhaps even a majority of European colonists) did not feel the need to alter their relationship with Britain. When contemplating the myth of American democracy, the reasons behind the lack of revolutionary ardor are not as compelling as their absence. It is the striking void of a truly democratic movement, even among European males, which debunks the overarching mythology concerning the formation of the United States from a "democratic revolution."[ii]

Another historical determinant of the revolution, heretofore alluded to, but not specifically addressed, is the culture of violence in American society leading up to the war. In their stunning history of American violence, historians Richard Hofstader and Michael Wallace document innumerable instances of intense violence during the pre-Revolutionary period (Hofstader & Wallace 1970). These ranged from bloody conflicts between religious groups (Ibid, pgs. 49, 56), to bread riots (Ibid, p. 109) to the slaughter of defenseless American Indians (Ibid, p. 270). The relatively common occurrence of violence, coupled with its widespread use and acceptance in colonial society, provided fertile ground for the conflict's beginnings. Additionally, this colonial American weakness for brute force also helps explain the atrocities committed against "loyalists" during the war itself.

Throughout the colonies, egregious violations were committed against colonists who either did not support the Revolution or sympathized with England. Laws were passed by colonial legislatures and local committees which made legal the seizure or expropriation of loyalist property (Simmons 1976, p. 372). Not to be outdone by the rebel authorities, pro-independence supporters systematically terrorized, threatened and tortured loyalists (Middlekauff 1982, p. 551-555). Once again, the instances were innumerable and included such incidents as the beating and torture of a 70-year-old parish clerk in Connecticut (Hofstader & Wallace 1970, p. 77), and the tarring and feathering of a Boston man which was attended by thousands, replete with a five-hour cart ride interspersed with whippings on a frigid winter evening (Ibid, p. 78). Most of the families whose homes were confiscated or destroyed never returned or received compensation for their losses. Thousands fled to Canada or England seeking refuge from the terror. The abuse showered on the loyalists by the "patriots" (while providing further evidence of America's undemocratic heritage) was also a harbinger because serious transgressions against individual civil rights in the name of "freedom" or "democracy" would be a hallmark domestic governmental policy during every ensuing American war.

The continental army and the local militias were comprised mostly of impoverished men (Perret 1989, p. 27) while the leaders of the troops and in the affairs of state came primarily from the elite.[iii] By the end of the war, it was the elite class which held power in all of America's ruling bodies (Middlekauf 1982, p. 650). Also by this time, the Native American population on the eastern seaboard had been essentially eradicated. There was a large, politically powerless slave (and non-slave) underclass to provide labor, and most importantly there was no imperial "master" dictating America's market practices or enforcing taxes. With such newly acquired military and financial power, coupled with a social structure lacking any real resemblance to a representative democracy, one would expect the ruling class to have rejoiced at its good fortune.

THE ARTICLES OF CONFEDERATION

If the powerful had been satisfied with their lot, there is a distinct possibility that the Articles of Confederation, rather than being an historical footnote, would still be the law of the land in the United States. But, according to many standard historical presentations, the Articles of Confederation failed absolutely as a mechanism for governance, and these shortcomings provided the genesis for the vaunted Constitution. The facts, however, tell a story which is far less halcyon.

Ratified in 1781, the Articles of Confederation framed a new national government prior to the British defeat. It was ratified by all of the colonies and established a federal government devoid of both executive and judicial branches. This confederation held that all of the states had an equal vote in national affairs regardless of their size. The members of this new body performed many governing functions, but could not levy taxes or regulate commerce on a national level. These two important exceptions can be seen as philosophically consistent with colonial aphorisms propagandized before and during the revolution which, in part, inspired the struggle against the British.

Most of the power in the Articles of Confederation was vested in the governments of each individual state, while the national government played more of a supporting role in exercising authority. To many people in the lower and middle classes of American society this system impressed them as sensible, in light of the recent war they had fought against the centralized, imperial British government. Conversely, some citizens, mostly of the elite class, found the Articles of Confederation wanting because of its lack of centralized power.

There were various types of people who desired to change the Articles of Confederation. There were those, like Alexander Hamilton, who, even before the Articles had a chance to fail or succeed, viewed this form of decentralized governance as vile. Others who joined the opposition to the Articles, whether driven by their own frustrations with the government, or through the strident writings of the Federalist campaign led by Hamilton, gradually grew disenchanted.

As a form of government, the Articles of Confederation did have flaws. A governing formula born of reaction to British rule, the Articles created a system that masqueraded as a national authority, but depended on the States for its implementation. For those who desired a fully state-centered federation, the Articles failed because the federal government had some important powers. For those who wanted a centralized government, it fell short in their desire for a nationalizing authority. Caught in a netherworld of two polarities, the Articles did not fully legitimize either of these two conflicting ideologies. When historians laud the virtues of the U.S. Constitution and vilify the Articles of Confederation, the conflicted birth of the latter is seldom considered. Nor is it mentioned that the period between the Treaty of Paris in the fall of 1783 (which marked the official birth of a national government) and the pro-centralization Constitutional Convention in the spring of 1787 was less than four years; scarcely enough time for any government to prove its efficacy.

A brief example of pro-Constitution mythology occurs in Noel B. Gerson's rendering of this period, *Free and Independent The Confederation of the United States 1781-1789*. In his text he exalts the Constitution, "It is the heart, and perhaps the soul as well, of a nation dedicated to liberty, justice, and equality." (Gerson 1970, p. 11) Of the Articles of Confederation he writes, "The trials the infant nation endured and the errors she made during the period of the confederation...were so numerous that they could scarcely be counted." (Gerson 1970, p. 12) In the mind of this sentimental historian, the Constitution, written by great men in an effort to save a broken people from inevitable suffering, and to protect "liberty, justice, and equality," became the "soul" of the nation.

The result of such a limited historical portrayal is twofold. The first being the obvious cultural propagandizing of America's Constitution as a system which saved the country from certain ruin, a perspective that the most patriotic of historians, honestly assessing the state of American affairs during this period, would have a difficult time proving. For although the new government had difficulties, the common portrayal that the country faced an imminent demise due to the shortcomings of the Articles, is at best a specious assertion. Secondly, and most pertinent in discussing the myth of democracy, is the stubborn fact that compared to the Constitution, the decentralized, locally powerful mechanisms of the Articles of Confederation far outdistanced the Constitution in representative democracy; precisely the attribute for which the latter is so lauded.

This is not to say that the Articles of Confederation exemplified representative democracy as we understand it today. As noted, a significant portion of the colonial population, blacks, women, poor whites, slaves, Native Americans, etc., enjoyed no more freedom under the auspices of the Articles than they had under British rule. However, it is a simple truth that on a strictly comparative basis to the Constitution, the Articles were more democratic.

THE "FOUNDING FATHERS" AND THEIR CONSTITUTION

In order to discern the Constitution's intent and to fully understand how far removed the mainstream portrayal of events is from its actual construction, one must look to its authors. Who were these lionized men? What inspired them to reconstruct the government after such a short period of time? And most importantly, were they truly concerned with democracy?

Before exploring the "Founding Fathers'" worldview and its relationship to our present form of government, a minor, albeit often historically overlooked fact, bears mentioning. The eventual ratification of the Constitution was technically illegal. According to the ratification law set forth in the Articles of Confederation, any amendment to its content required the consent of every state. Prior to concluding the proceedings of the Constitutional Convention, the Founding Fathers, knowing in advance that they would be unable to muster universal support for their new government, decided that only nine of the states were needed to ratify the Constitution.

Lawbreaking of this sort was not solely the product of their hubris, but a tacit admission of their substantial power and influence in the era's political arena, and was symbolic of the illegitimate government they wished to form.

The individuals who gathered in Philadelphia for the Constitutional Convention were men of wealth, power and prestige (Burns 1991, p. 32). As we now know, the Conventioneers did much more than "amend" the Articles of Confederation; they wrote an entirely new document which called for a government so radically dissimilar to the Articles that historians have written volumes about the process in an attempt to discern the motives of the authors.

It is important to juxtapose the social positions of the Constitution's authors with their motives because it forms a debate from which two competing conclusions can be drawn. The first is that if these men acted with some self-interest, it was only a product of their humanity; they saw the Constitution primarily as an effort to save the country from ruin. A contrary opinion, popularized by historian Charles Beard, was that money and property concerns, rather than nationalistic altruism, played the pivotal role at the Convention.

If these early American statesman had indeed sacrificed themselves so unselfishly for the benefit of the fledgling nation, then surely they deserve the accolades of the mythmakers. Their behavior would mark perhaps the first, last, and only occasion when a gathering of powerful men made decisions completely beyond the influence of power and money. This would classify the Convention as nothing short of a miraculous historical anomaly (which many believe it is).

The prospect of these men reinventing the American government on the basis of property and money, exclusive of the desire for greater control, is also faulty. This line of reasoning proposes separating these two eternal human desires-money and power- and does not clarify their motives in any meaningful way.

Ultimately, the Conventioneers concerned themselves with all of the aforementioned issues. The proof of the power and resource consolidation lay in the laws established by the Constitution, which created a federal militia, a central bank, and the federal regulation of trade and taxation. The revelatory disparity between the Articles of Confederation and the Constitution is the drastic shift in control of national money and power transactions to the federal government from the states. The mythology surrounding the Founding Fathers' "sacrifice" for the nation has persisted, as the Constitution, after more than two hundred years, remains (not without tumultuous struggle) the law of the United States.

Perhaps it would be enlightening to delve more deeply into the opinions of several Founding Fathers regarding their thoughts on democracy. Following the Convention and prior to the fight for ratification, Alexander Hamilton, a Conventioneer, the Treasury Secretary under Washington and one of the leading proponents for ratification said the Constitution had:

> *The good will of the commercial interest throughout the States, which will give all its efforts to the establishment of a government capable of regulating, protecting, and extending the commerce of the Union. The good will of most men of property in the several States, who wish a government of the Union able to protect them against domestic violence, and the depredations which the democratic spirit is apt to make on property... (Mason 1956, p. 266)*

In arguing for the ratification of the Constitution, in Federalist Paper number 10, James Madison, a Conventioneer, inaugural Congressman and future President wrote:

> *...democracies have ever been spectacles of turbulence and contention; have ever been found incompatible with personal security or the rights of property; and have been in general as short in their lives as they have been violent in their deaths.*

During the debate over the new national legislature, Conventioneer Edmund Randolph argued, "The Democratic licentiousness of the State Legislatures proved the necessity of a firm Senate. The object of this 2nd branch is to control the democratic branch of the National Legislature (Mason, 1956, p. 216)."[iv] Eldbridge Gerry, a Conventioneer from Massachusetts thought of democracy as, "...the worst...of all political evils (Mason, 1956, p. 240)." John Dickinson argued at the Convention that restricting suffrage to white male freeholders was a "...defense against the dangerous influence of those multitudes without property and without principle...(Mason 1956, p. 237)." Pierce Butler of South Carolina, in forwarding his point that when accounting for a state's population slaves should represent one person (the eventual, cynical compromise had blacks represented as 3/5 of a person), summed up the attitude of the Conventioneers when he stated that, "...an equal representation ought to be allowed for them [slaves] in a Government which was instituted principally for the protection of property, and was itself to be supported by property (Mason 1956, p. 232)."

These quotations demonstrate the Founding Fathers' lack of faith and undisguised contempt for democracy. Their primary concern was to establish a national, centralized government that would protect their financial and property interests, which they construed to represent the fundamental qualities of liberty. Historian Richard Hofstadter aptly summarizes their outlook, "The Founding Fathers thought that the liberty with which they were most concerned was menaced by democracy. In their minds liberty was linked not to democracy but to property (Bishop & Hendel 1948, p. 102-103)." The sad truth was that these men, many of whom had so skillfully propagandized the wonders of democracy to foment the Revolution, were sympathetic to and only truly understood the mechanisms of the dispatched British Government, and were not comfortable with the threat of an actual democracy even in a limited form. And so the United States inherited from these men an amalgamated governmental structure, based partly on British common law, and partly on their need to protect their political and monetary holdings. This amalgam also proved to be amply devoid of democratic mechanisms.

We have already seen that the Articles of Confederation were unlawfully superseded in the drive to ratify the new constitution. The Founding Fathers knew they would have a difficult time passing their document through the very state legislatures they aimed to disenfranchise. So in addition to declaring that only nine states (out of thirteen) were needed to ratify, they decreed that ratification be conducted by specially appointed state conventions, rather than directly by the legislatures. In so doing, they promised themselves some insulation from the "democratic licentiousness of the state legislatures," and a significantly greater chance at ratification.

When the general public became aware of the Constitution's content, a heated debate commenced. The debate for and against ratification divided the population largely along class lines, with the wealthier merchants and lawyers in support of the Constitution and the poorer classes allied against ratification (Caldwell 1925, p. 238). Propaganda for adoption, now enshrined in the Federalist Papers, had the support of the elite. The pro-Federalist movement was better financed and organized than the opposition. Although he was a member of the elite, Thomas Jefferson flatly refuted one of the main charges leveled by the Federalist propagandists: that the Articles of Confederation were leading the country towards anarchy (supposedly evidenced by Shay's Rebellion in Massachusetts). In the midst of the Constitutional debate, he wrote, "Yet where does this anarchy exist? Where except in the single instance of Massachusetts?" (Mason 1956, p. 247)

In 1787, the year the debate over ratification began, it is estimated that the majority of the population was opposed to ratification (Parrington 1927, p. 283-284). It is also likely that without the property qualifications for the state conventions, the Constitution would not have passed (Caldwell 1925, p. 239). Ultimately, the premeditation of the Founding Fathers paid dividends. The Constitution was not ratified by all of the states, but was implemented in 1789, without unanimous support. If the Founding Fathers had allowed for a popular referendum (even with the votes of blacks, women, etc. excluded), it certainly would have failed miserably.

The Constitution was a victory of power and wealth over citizens calling for democratic institutions. The new document rescinded the power of the common voting citizens in that it allowed them to vote only for candidates to the House of Representatives and this right was checked by other non-elected officials: the President, the Supreme Court and the Senate. All of these bodies were indirectly elected or appointed; the real meaning behind "checks and balances." Perhaps more importantly, its laws established the legal precedent for future generations of American militarists and industrialists.

THE BILL OF RIGHTS

The one remaining refuge for those who cling to the myth of democracy is the Bill of Rights. Before pointing to a couple of key factors which seriously derail the Bill of Rights' historic validity, it must be noted that the Founding Fathers were contemptuous enough of civil liberties to make no mention of them in the Constitution. There are those who would argue that the intention of the Fathers was to leave such questions to the whims of the individual states.

It certainly seems odd that the Conventioneers, who so assiduously worked at designing a government which shifted military, financial and legislative control to the federal level, would leave this question to the states. What this omission truly indicates is the Conventioneers' disregard for the protection of universal civil liberties. It reminds us again that these men were not interested in establishing a democratic system. Ratification of these amendments foreshadowed future manifestations of genuine American democracy in that they sprang from widespread, popular resistance to the undemocratic actions of the federal authorities. A popular outcry forced the Founding Fathers hand.

As we shall see, the Bill of Rights, even after 200 years of existence does not guarantee a democratic American society. There are always more tools at the disposal of the powerful to counteract the threat of a truly democratic society, but what of the Bill of Rights at the time of its ratification? Did this not represent some kind of democratic achievement after two centuries of American progress? The response to such a hopeful assessment is negative. It was not the content of the amendments which suffered (freedom of the press, freedom of religious worship, freedom to peaceably gather, etc.) but the amendments themselves which buckled under the weight of a fundamentally undemocratic government in no way prepared to honor these lofty principles. Aside from the visible condition of the population's majority, i.e. slaves, Native Americans, women, non-freeholder white males, each having no opportunity or recourse to enjoy these privileges, the government's effort to restrict the Bill of Rights began almost immediately. In 1790, before the Bill of Rights was even added to the Constitution, Congress passed a naturalization act that excluded non-white and Native American citizenship (Takaki 1993, p. 80). And in 1798, Congress passed laws which came to be known as the Alien and Sedition Acts. These laws violated the civil liberties-theoretically ensured by the Bill of Rights-of all Americans. Written ostensibly in reaction to increased tensions with the French, they permitted the President to deport aliens in times of peace and forbid people from criticizing Congress or the President (Burns 1991, p. 125-126).

From this brief overview of the United States' first years of existence, it is evident that by any definition, the country, even following a "democratic" revolution and the defeat of an imperial monarchy, in no way resembled a representative democracy. Universal suffrage was absent, as was the idea of protecting civil liberties. We have likewise observed, in the power and financial consolidation perpetuated by the illegally and undemocratically ratified Constitution, the absence of the republican principle whereby the authorities' right to exercise power emanates from the consent of the governed. Clearly, these men, in circumventing the Articles of Confederation and forwarding a set of laws so insulated from the "multitudes without property or principle," placed small significance on the consent of the governed. Their intent was a contrary attempt to systematically protect the propertied and powerful from the corrosive influence of the masses.

Much as Jefferson's Declaration of Independence would forever remain a stubborn thorn in the side of the American authorities, so too was to be the role of the Bill of Rights. Born of a democratic reaction to the fundamentally non-democratic Constitution, the multifarious future battles over the Bill of Rights served as a constant reminder of America's inability to acknowledge its inhabitants' basic civil liberties.

The myth that the United States threw off its imperial British chains to emerge as a new democracy has never become a reality. America's mythmakers, in professing a culture of democracy, merely misnamed the animal. The behavior of the nascent U.S. government and the first ruling elites, reveals its true nature. This latent hypocrisy between a propagandized ideal and actual behavior is in many ways the defining characteristic of the United States government. It is explicitly the corruption and illegitimacy of America's early ideals that cultivated the imperial disease and corresponding mythology that has led directly to the decrepit state of democracy in modern American society.

2

HELPING THE PEOPLE BELIEVE

"Them sailing on their evil trip,
blast off on their space ship,
a million miles from reality,
no care for you no care for me..."

– BOB MARLEY
So Much Trouble in the World

"For slavery looks much like freedom when the master is never seen."

– WILL DURANT

"I pledge allegiance to the flag of the United States of America and
to the republic for which it stands, one nation under God,
indivisible, with liberty and justice for all."

– UNITED STATES PLEDGE OF ALLEGIANCE

"A really efficient totalitarian state would be one in which the
all-powerful executive of political bosses and their army of managers
control a population of slaves who do not have to be coerced, because they
love their servitude. To make them love it is the task assigned, in present
day totalitarian states, to ministries of propaganda, newspaper editors,
and schoolteachers. But their methods are still cruel and unscientific..."

– ALDOUS HUXLEY

From the collection of useless information imparted to me during my thirteen year American public education, there is next to nothing I can quote verbatim aside from the Pledge of Allegiance. My remembrance is not based on any
affinity for its content; I cited it largely by rote, and as a teenager viewed it with
apathy if not a little suspicion. Rather, it was the sheer number of recitations
which fixed it indelibly in my psyche. The Pledge of Allegiance as an incantation
provides a concrete example of a combined myth/propaganda program

designed to engender support for a particular regime. It serves as myth in that it urges the speaker to accept historical misrepresentations i.e., "liberty and justice for all" at face value, with no qualifying explanation. The Pledge of Allegiance also functions as efficient propaganda because it is a current, deliberate campaign, implemented by authority for the sole purpose of instilling patriotism and obedience. As part of their daily instruction, schoolchildren in public institutions are required to utter these sentiments without debate.

Although the Pledge of Allegiance is an exceedingly obvious example of both myth and propaganda mechanisms, there are countless other forms of such manipulation. What makes myth or propaganda damaging is their use by authorities as tools of coercion. If the rulers' primary objective is to have a group commit, ignore, and directly or indirectly support destructive or immoral behavior under the guise of conduct generally regarded as positive (like freedom, humanitarianism or democracy), then myth and propaganda create negative consequences. This coercion is not viewed by those in power as vile or destructive because their own interests are at stake. There is, however, a profound difference between the historical and contemporary manifestations of this phenomenon. While the myths and propaganda spun by the powerful even a hundred years ago often proved harmful or potentially fatal to their minions, the stakes are now much higher. In the age of nuclear weapons and in the impending environmental catastrophe spawned by Western consumption and globalization, we now have threats, supported by myths and propaganda, that may prove to be the undoing of earthly existence.

MYTHS AS A TOOL OF CORRUPTION

Myths are fictional, descriptive anecdotes, which often serve as shared cultural barometers. Retelling stories binds people together through religion, communal morality, sacrifice, or shared causes, with a subsidiary purpose of providing social cues. Such cues do not, by default, impart unfavorable legacies on societies. Myths frequently embody ideals to which human beings have aspired for centuries.

Because myths customarily retain so much universal resonance with humanity, societal leaders often misuse them. The urge to abuse myths is alluring due to their strength in galvanizing public support for furthering the power and monetary interests of the few. If, for example, a leader were to tell his subjects, "We fight the war to protect our national sovereignty and way of life," it is certainly more effective than stating, "We are attacking these people to bring more resources and area under my control." The first example calls upon shared sacrifice and unity while the latter merely admits to selfishness. One rarely hears the truth from mythmakers, and more notably, they often call upon the shared experience of the masses as justification for slaughter.

Beyond the obvious personal benefits a ruler or ruling class derives from usurping myths, the expropriation plays an equally pivotal role in the smooth operation of the state. However, only in power-corrupted societies can widespread implementation of this negative mythmaking be possible, and it is common in such societies that almost every myth called upon by the authorities to engender patriotism, or to glorify governmental behavior, actually ends up helping to enslave, injure or eradicate large segments of the population.

It is also the case in corrupt societies that the forces at work are so potent that many non-governmental players (who often reap no benefit from their repetition), spend an abundance of energy endorsing these negative myths. Unofficial parroting by civilians solidifies a lesson of power: those in power must, especially in ostensibly democratic societies, first sing a lullaby which placates the masses before they can begin following a course of exploitation.

PROPAGANDA AS A TOOL OF CORRUPTION

All of the aforementioned qualities indicate why myths appeal so strongly to authorities; but what of propaganda, does it too have similar functions? Propaganda generally differs from myth in that it reacts to contemporary stimuli. The intention of the propagandist is to convince others to adopt his or her perspective through whatever means at their disposal. Even in nominally democratic societies the effects of propaganda are inherently mitigated by the nature of democracy. In a democratic culture, the wishes of the propagandists can be somewhat checked and deflated by the actions of a vested populace.

Unchecked and unconstrained propaganda which dictates the behavior of a population is the clearest sign that a society either never was democratic or has become democratically bankrupt. As with myths, propaganda in undemocratic societies aims to control or convince a population to unequivocally support the decisions of the authorities. It behooves the rulers to try to employ this indoctrination to a level that the words or ideas become commonly accepted and repeated by the masses, who then (if all goes well) come to believe that the opinions of the propagandist are personal beliefs rather than misinformation. Once the instruction reaches such a level - with large swaths of the population parroting the party line - the job of the propagandists becomes much easier. At this point, the mere mention of a catchword, like "terrorist," is all that is needed to produce the desired effect. To achieve this kind of success, rulers and their propagandists must also have at their disposal the means of mass communication. Without the compliance of or control over the media, their message would be less widespread and therefore less effective.

Unlike myths, propaganda has few positive attributes. Whereas myths can help bond a community through shared experience, propaganda almost always results in convincing or coercing an individual or society to act or think in a particular politically motivated manner. This fact alone does not mean that propaganda is always evil, but it points to the potential for its abuse by those with power. Perhaps the only saving grace for propaganda is when it is used to promote a just cause. But even this possibility carries snares as the judgment of "just" lies always with the propagandist. Corrupt authorities adore the use of propaganda, because it is an even more effective manipulation tool than myth in furthering self-serving goals.

It is precisely the connection between myth and propaganda which gives full bloom to the true nature of these phenomena. Without a thorough understanding of the symbiosis between myth and propaganda, it is impossible to appreciate the ramifications of America's democratic mythology. The use of time inviolably cements the relationship between myth and propaganda. Propaganda such as the Pledge of Allegiance would lose all of its potency, and perhaps more relevantly, would be devoid of meaning if it were not based on the American myth of "liberty and justice for all." The myth's invocation in the Pledge guarantees that its meaning carries cultural and historical cues which give it contemporary significance. Likewise, the myth of American "liberty and justice for all" would be lost if it were not repeated and enforced in a cultural setting like the public school.

Examples proving the interdependence of myth and propaganda are not always blatant, but when implemented by authorities, the two feed on each other for their survival. And so it goes that rulers or ruling classes who look to use myth and propaganda to their advantage, steadfastly apply and fully comprehend the intricacies of this relationship. They know that employing one without the other can seriously diminish the legitimacy and power of the message they wish to convey. After identifying any effective myth espoused by a corrupt authority, the corresponding piece of propaganda often becomes clearer and helps form a coherent whole.

AMERICAN DEMOCRACY

Turning again to focus on the United States we must scrutinize the legacy of America's democratic deficit and how this affects the present-day U.S. government. Many people, both at home and abroad, profess to believe in the principle of democracy and hold up the United States government as a paragon of democratic success. Before undertaking a status check on the condition of American democracy, I would first like to briefly explain my personal perception of the dangers involved in certain definitions of the word.

Excepting democracy's potency as a propaganda tool, let's take the position of those who prefer the strictly American application of the word. The people who share this perspective can be said to be adherents of the Representative

School of Democracy. They believe that any person, in any country, who has the right to vote for the majority of their legislators and executives, and is granted a certain amount of civil liberties, lives in a democracy. According to this School, the power to vote is considered the defining characteristic which acts as a democratic bell-weather. There may be an unending list of major and minor governmental offenses, lapses, abuses of power, or even wholesale corruption, yet none of these factors, in the eyes of the Representative theorist, undermine the power of the vote. The obvious problem with the Representative theory of democracy is that the voter is left with very few options when the power structure becomes so ensconced that it is immune to any serious change via the vote.

In addition to electing politicians for local and state offices,[i] American citizens (now including minorities, the poor and women) also elect politicians to serve in two of the three main branches of the federal government. Representative theorists believe that this makes America a democracy. Passive democracy of this sort is just what those who benefit the most from this reality would have a citizen believe. They proselytize that voting is the crux of citizenship and hope that this will assuage any unsettling suspicions a person harbors that he or she may not be participating in true democracy. The incalculable benefits reaped by the authorities through the practice of this Representative theory provide the best sign that this form of government has corrupted the deeper meaning of democracy.

The current manifestation of this form of governance finds its roots in Washingtonian-era America. Even though we have discerned the Founding Fathers' contempt for democracy, they recognized (primarily through their desire to keep white men of property invested with the reigns of control) that a semblance of citizen participation in the government was necessary. Similar to modern American rulers, the original American authorities felt that the type of government they established was, if not a democracy, a participatory government. Present-day American authorities' belief in representative "democracy" is therefore directly descended from the restricted vote begun by the first U.S. officials. If pressed, today's politicians could actually point to America's ignominious past as an example of how the United States has evolved from a relatively undemocratic nation into a more democratic one. The irony of course is that these very same individuals enthusiastically employ the historical myth of democracy to their advantage as an example of shared greatness.

The real democratic process in the United States has nothing to do with its politicians, present or past. True to all empires' conflicted and flawed natures, the functionaries of the United States have generally opposed democracy, emancipation and suffrage. In the struggle for universal suffrage it has been the democratic actions of common citizens which forced the hand of the politicians towards recognition of individual sovereignty. It took the disenfranchised citizens of the United States more than 170 years to receive the right to vote and equal legal protection. These rights were granted only following tumultuous conflict. From the Civil War, to the suffrage, labor and civil rights movements, hundreds of thousands lost their lives, all in a popular struggle for recognition against a government opposed to popular will.

The conflict fought by the masses of oppressed citizens for governmental recognition of their basic humanity is one of the great ironies of American history. The people whom the Founding Fathers most dishonored (and gave the fewest rights to) were foremost in forcing more democracy onto this undemocratic system. Conversely, the people favored by the Founding Fathers have consistently undermined the democratic process, denied citizens' civil rights and attempted to sustain a power structure that benefits the few over the many. While oppression is the historical legacy of America's ruling class, democracy remains the legacy of its common citizens.

Such a backwards condition is instructive as to the operation of American society, for while the standard recitation of American history credits the various presidents, congressmen, Supreme Court Justices and the Constitution as the source of democratic tradition, just the reverse is true. The Constitution was devised as a weapon against democracy and the Presidents, et al. ceded power (and then received democratic accolades from historians) only when compelled by exterior forces. Examples such as Lincoln's opposition to slavery only after the southern secession from the union or Kennedy's and Johnson's concern for civil rights following years of widespread popular resistance are repeated throughout U.S. history.

Still, under the definition of democracy put forth in the previous chapter, it would appear that the contemporary American government now fulfills most requirements of a democratic society. There is universal suffrage, people are (in theory) protected equally under the law, and there may be a few elected officials who would acknowledge that their right to govern is granted by the citizens and not pre-ordained. Although none of these characteristics are faultless (no large organization of flawed human beings could ever be perfect) they certainly point to a long-wayward government finally on the road to an imperfect, but operational, representative democracy. The reasons that America does not resemble anything like an imperfect democracy--even though it superficially meets some democratic requirements--lie in its history. As the citizens busied themselves with fighting the wars of, doing the work of, and struggling for their rights against the government, those in control were busy doing what they do best: consolidating power, money and resources. And much like an abusive person, vitiated governments and societies do not mend well on their own accord.

In modern American society this inherited sickness manifests itself in several relevant, albeit debilitating ways. Since we are concerned foremost with the relative ineffectuality of mechanisms which would normally signify the presence of democracy, we must look at institutions through the lens of these elements, i.e. basic human rights, voting, etc. The first example to consider is the proliferation of non-elected governmental organizations in 20th century America. When examining a representative sample of these creations, it is vital to note that their presence alone is not necessarily nefarious, they become so when juxtaposed with the tremendous suffering and poverty of citizens from whose money and compliance they are made possible.

NON-ELECTED BODIES AND
THE MODERN DEMOCRATIC MYTH

Because militaries are common to most countries and because an entire subsequent chapter is dedicated to American militarism, I will not at the moment focus on it in its entirety, but a brief look at the American nuclear weapons program provides a suitable first example of a debilitating undemocratic institution.

Since the founding of the United States' nuclear arsenal, the government has spent trillions of dollars on developing, maintaining and employing these weapons of mass destruction. The questions here are not whether these weapons were scientifically inevitable (therefore better that we have them), nor whether they provide security by protecting us from a nuclear attack, but, in what tangible manner have these weapons and the accompanying expenditures, bettered American citizens' lives? Nuclear arms have in no way benefited the average citizen and have usurped almost incomprehensible amounts of taxpayer funds without so much as one directly cast vote in their favor. Regarding what beneficial results these funds could have been spent on, an appropriate gauge is that during the period from 1940-1996, the U.S. government spent 5.5 trillion dollars (in constant 1996 dollars) on its nuclear program compared to 3.3 trillion combined on health and education programs (Schwartz, 1998).

Another poignant example of American governmental malfeasance is the National Aeronautics and Space Agency or NASA. The advent of NASA coincided with the Cold War and essentially amounted to a space colonization race with the Russians. For many Americans, NASA is a sacred entity. Much becomes lost in peoples' exuberance for putting men on the moon, sending probes to the outer reaches of the solar system and building space stations. The point here is not to denigrate these activities but to shed light on their relationship to the lives of America's poor. Any controlling authority that would spend billions of taxpayer dollars on a program that provides no relief for its suffering citizens beyond fleeting glimpses of faraway realities is suspect. It would be shortsighted to argue that NASA's pursuits serve only as a propagandized distraction, or to contend that the intent behind NASA is purely licentious (although its function as a wing of the military often goes unmentioned). It would likewise be shortsighted to claim that governmental conduct through institutions like NASA represents the workings of a democratic society.

The final sample of a non-elected, undemocratic 20th century American institution is the Central Intelligence Agency. Like its numerous compatriot authoritarian "security" organizations, the FBI, the ATF, the NSA, etc., the official reasons behind the CIA's existence revolves around notions of protecting and promoting American governmental interests in its relations with outside countries and foreign nationals. The dark truth of the CIA's mandate and how it has used taxpayer funds is far more nefarious than its official purpose. The agency has both willfully and mistakenly led the country into wars (Vietnam, Iraq), worked to overthrow foreign governments (including Chile, Nicaragua, and Cuba), and helped sustain brutal dictatorships (Indonesia, Iran, Iraq). All this came at the cost of countless lives and tremendous suffering at home and abroad. If this were not a strong enough indictment, the CIA has regularly failed to achieve the goals it established for itself. The CIA's actions have engendered a deep hatred among many peoples, both foreign and domestic, which in turn has spawned terrorist attacks against American civilians. Although the CIA's actions have fomented a great deal of anger that generates retaliatory violence, they generally benefit from the subsequent need for heightened "security." All of which dictates the United States' hypothetical need for the agency and has paved the way for laws like 1996's "Anti-terrorism" bill, the USA Patriot Act, and the Homeland Security Act, that in turn further restrict Americans' individual rights and allocate billions of taxpayer dollars with more such bills sure to come. Ironically, as the CIA toiled to overthrow democratically elected foreign governments, the poor residents of its own "democratic" country experienced little improvements in their lives. [ii]

Beyond propping up American imperial, corporate and military interests, to what extent has the average United States citizen benefited from the CIA's,

NASA's or nuclear arms presence in the government? If we look at U.S. poverty statistics (see previous endnote) and juxtapose them with the benefits derived by American corporate, governmental and military interests through these institutions, the equation is simple: the decline of the Soviet Empire has, with the help of these organizations, left the United States Empire (and its subsidiary countries, i.e. Great Britain, China, Israel) the indisputable master of the globe without the slightest lessening of its citizens' impoverishment.

One may argue that while these institutions may be undemocratic, they are still run by elected officials at the very top of the command chain. But, in the face of continued mass suffering, little is effectively done by elected officials regarding reform, let alone dismantling these operations in favor of human services. The reality is that a prudent review would occur only in a democratic society.

DEMOCRATS AND REPUBLICANS AS DEMOCRATIC MYTH

The myth of democracy is a great passion of many Democratic and Republican politicians. They have come to believe that they are the representatives of a historically and contemporarily great democracy. In their campaign speeches and in their speeches before Congress they summon images of the United States' blessed "democratic" heritage. What they fail to see (or perhaps choose to ignore) is that their participation in American politics through sanctioned parties has kept - and continues to keep - the United States from being even moderately democratic.

The stranglehold that the Democrats and Republicans have over the electoral process epitomizes the symbolic and literal realization of democratic bankruptcy in American society. What the elected officials profess to stand for is largely beside the point. The presence of only two perspectives on any issue constitutes an oligarchy, not a democracy.

On a very real level, all divergent views have to be included in the ideology of the ruling parties. If not, then the viewpoint has no place in a political discussion. Asking a ruling party to submit to or concur with a truly dissident view, would be unthinkable. Plainly, for the Democrats or Republicans to implement actual reform or elimination of NASA, the nuclear arsenal, or the CIA, would be to undermine their own power. These entities (and others like them) were created to consolidate Democratic and Republican control of the political process. Although eliminating one of these undemocratic institutions could partially alleviate the discomfort of people they govern, it would be detrimental to their own interests. The two-party system has the effect of guaranteeing that questions fundamental to issues of American inequality never enter into the political arena.

These parties have become eerily similar over time. Just as they depend on the democratic myth for partial justification, so do they depend on each other. The propaganda surrounding their antagonism for each other helps prop up the phony play. They implore the voters to become involved in their mock debates and they profess distaste for one another through positions on issues that they claim as core beliefs. Perhaps the charade has gone on for so long that they actually believe the other party is the enemy. It would be amusing, however, if one party did ultimately rule over the other. If America became a one-party system, all of the pretense of alleged democracy would disappear. With two choices to vote for, one can still pretend a decision is being made, but with only one party even the most domesticated citizen may become suspicious. In fact, if the American populace does not articulate this scenario, the evidence is ample that most people recognize that voting in national elections is irrelevant. Historically, voting percentages in the U.S. have been fairly anemic, but participation in Presidential elections has declined steadily over the last few decades to the point that only half of the electorate bothers to go to the polls.

It must also be said that the similarities in the two parties' platforms have become almost completely blurred since the demise of the Soviet Union. [iii] Now that the "leftist threat" is gone, the pro-corporate, militaristic power designs of the two parties has, to a large degree, been unmasked. The result is a political spectrum that consists of an attempt to see which party can best maintain the status quo. Incidentally, this phenomenon has taken place in other parts of the world as well, with formerly left-leaning European parties (i.e. the British Labor Party) co-opting the pro-corporate approach of their former Conservative party foes. There are those who would argue that America's political process results directly from the desires of the people and that it is these desires, not the imposition of the parties on the American psyche, which have determined the current paradigm. The quick rebuttal is that it would be difficult to tell: two-party politics have been the norm since the first Constitutional government onward. [iv] Barring any real threat to the parties' hegemony it would be hard responding to this "chicken or the egg" hypothesis. One thing does remain clear. The parties' primary focus is not on serving the people, but on maintaining the primacy of their power. This kind of arrogant self-fulfillment distinguishes dictatorships and oligarchies from democracies.

The myth of democracy, although a potent cornerstone of the United States' two-party system, does not alone carry enough power to allow the American authorities to continue ruling in the manner they do. The suffering propagated by the government affects the working and under classes the hardest. The taxpayer resources gobbled up by misspent governmental funds has an unpleasant ripple effect that pervades many aspects of American life. It can be as simple as a pang in a rich person's heart as they walk by a homeless man on their way to work; the signs are ceaselessly evident (in everything from vast wealth inequalities, to the lack of health insurance for millions of Americans, to millions of children growing up in poverty) and prey upon the conscience of the nation. It is through the coupling of the democratic myth and propaganda that the rich and powerful are able to continue their reign of injustice.

HELPING THE PEOPLE BELIEVE

To be influential, propaganda needs other factors beyond self-reference to support its message. It needs a cultural context for people to internalize its meaning. For instance, advertisers cannot merely claim, "buy this car;" they must appeal to a broader, deeper instinct, i.e., "buy this car, it will increase your stature among your peers." The same is true for the government and its control structures. Their message carries no weight without the force of shared myths or mores. Propaganda and myth are most effective when they are defined through each other.

Before entering into a more specific examination of present day propaganda devices, let's contemplate an example of the blurring that takes place between myth and propaganda. The American myth of individualism, sometimes known as the "rags to riches" phenomenon frames the individual as the creator of personal wealth and prosperity. This myth finds its origins in the United States' frontier mentality when American families trudged out on their own to make a life for themselves faced with the most grueling circumstances. The same myth persists in stories of poor urban immigrants who arrived on America's shores with nothing but obstacles facing them, yet through determination and hard work, they fought their way to prosperity.

The debate here is not whether such things occurred (although there is abundant evidence that systemic class mobility in America was and is very limited: McMurrer & Sawhill 1998, p. 35), but rather in what ways does this myth affect modern American attitudes, and in what ways does it benefit the authorities' desires? Although Americans' disdain for the poor stems partly from this myth of individualism, this perspective usually reveals itself at a deeper level in the American psyche which reasons, "These people need to help themselves. There is only so much others can do for them." And echoes further that if people remain poor following efforts to improve their lot then it is their own fault; the logic is that the American system can only provide a boost to the poor and can never be a hindrance. This viewpoint is actually encouraged by many politicians and is such a powerful propaganda tool that citizens have supported legislation such as the 1996 welfare "reform" bill which diminished funding allocated to the poor. This occurred even though all social spending (which includes many more programs than welfare) in 1995 represented 17.1% of the gross national product, a pittance when compared with expenditures of similar nations (Hacker 2002, p. 13-15). In this instance, what the interface of myth and propaganda accomplishes is to focus the population's attention on excessive government spending for the poor, and, by extension, the failure of the poor to help themselves. It transforms what is a complicated societal issue into a satisfyingly simplistic one. The propaganda would not be useful to the authorities without the aid of individualism as attendant myth. Without this crutch, the authorities would have a difficult time encouraging the retraction of money and services from desperate people.

This "pull themselves up by their own bootstraps" paradigm shifts the responsibility and the focus away from the government and onto the marginalized individual.[v] This may be appropriate and would not be propaganda if the government was not overly involved in peoples' lives by spending hundreds of billions a year of collected taxes propping up their own power interests in the form of corporate tax relief, the military, NASA, the CIA, and other pork barrel projects. Any genuine competition is predicated on some measure of fair play among the participants. How can individualism exist in a country where the rulers have already co-opted the power and spent the money excised from the people before the game has commenced? What a glorious vision it would be to witness the government try to pull itself up without tax money or the undemocratic institutions that support the regime.

American "individualism" vacillates between propaganda and myth due to the difficulty in placing the phenomenon solidly within the context of past events. Propaganda mechanisms often depend on myths for legitimacy, but it has a base necessity to inundate a population with behavior modification messages. Consistent with the characteristics of collective myths, layers upon layers of propaganda efforts have been waged by the United States government throughout the country's existence. Below are a few topical, highly damaging propaganda campaigns.

When leaders instill xenophobia into the population, it helps further their control. In America it provides the ruling class with a shared enemy and a unifying cultural cause, all of which facilitates commitment of the most heinous crimes in the name of righteous, justifiable behavior. It is not desirable to tell the citizenry that murder and mayhem are perpetuated to expand the control of the authorities. This sentiment must be dressed in clothes of enlightenment or tendered as a threat of invasion, because empires at their core are obese manifestations of militarism, xenophobia encourages citizens to support the military through the manipulation of fear.

Fear of others implies that the fear is directed externally, but that is not always the case. Hitler's propaganda war against the Jews or America's propaganda war against the Japanese during World War II are both examples of internal xenophobia. Historically, American rulers have waged countless propaganda wars against sections of the populace (take for example, black Americans, Native Americans, Mexicans, leftists, anarchists, communists, Muslims, the poor, immigrants, etc.) all of which have served the dual purpose of influencing the populace and taking the focus off the authorities' actions. It is once again important to realize that these internal campaigns are always directed at relatively powerless minorities because they are most efficient when aimed at constituencies which cannot effectively defend themselves.

As for external fears, the propagandized fear of the Soviet Union coincided (not surprisingly) with the rapid expansion of the American Empire. Thus, as the American authorities sold the public on the idea of the Soviet menace, they were busy creating the tools and consolidating the power of the United States' Empire. Predictably, the Cold War fomented the greatest expansion of American imperialism.

The fear of the Soviet Union was not primarily ideological; it too was ruled by a dominant, pro (state-run) business, militaristic, one party (rather than two) system. It was not enough to scare U.S. civilians into thinking they would have only one party rather than two control them, so the propaganda focused on ideas of democracy and freedom,[vi] most successfully linked to one's ability to own private property. In actuality, the truth beneath this surface ideological struggle was a simple power and propaganda contest between two massive empires.

The collapse of the Soviet Union posed a real threat to the United States' propaganda machine, which had been rooted for generations in spreading a fear of communism. All of the institutions that had been created to "protect" or promote American interests over communist interests, suddenly lost their purpose. The dirty secret that the U.S. military, space, nuclear, and security organization buildup was as much a power grab as it was a response to comparable Soviet efforts was easily propagandized as a communist counterweight.

Evidence that the government and America's undemocratic Cold War organizations internalized this secret surfaced almost immediately. Following the breakup of the U.S.S.R. into newly independent nations, the new threats to American interests were suddenly "rogue" states and radical Muslims. Accordingly, the new Powell doctrine (based on the Pentagon's 1991 *Base Force Review*), preached that the United States needed to be able to fight two simultaneous wars. Such quick justifications and a bold new propaganda war rapidly closed the tiny crack which had allowed some citizens to begin wondering why hundreds of billions of their yearly tax dollars were still necessary for such costly programs. Persistent ruinous spending, cynical military escapades (see Iraq, Columbia, Afghanistan, Serbia) and the lack of a rational discussion about any of these bodies since the passing of the Soviet Empire, attest to the malleability of state propaganda and indicate that the aforementioned crack may have been permanently sealed.

How can this information be effectively conveyed to the public in a country where a privately owned press controls the dispersal of information and freedom of the press is guaranteed by the Bill of Rights? The answer lies in one of the United States' most well-manicured flaws: the mass media exists and operates firmly within the confines of the country's dominant power structures.

We have seen that the prospect of relying upon the Democrats or Republicans to eradicate or reform undemocratic institutions they have created is ludicrous. The same theory holds true for the media conglomerates, all of which benefit greatly from America's economic and military power. As it stands now, the number of organizations that control the news and information disseminated to the American public has consolidated and continues to grow smaller with the 50 dominant media conglomerates in 1983 being reduced to 5 by 2003 (Bagdikian 2004). These few corporations are huge oligarchies that make a tremendous amount of money as the direct result of the United States' influence and wield an extraordinary amount of sway over the citizenry's mindset. From a purely physiological point of view, the investment these corporations have in challenging basic doctrines of the Empire is minute. It would be bad for their health.

Much of the mass media criticism in the United States has observed the above situation and has correctly noted that with further consolidation the urge to criticize the control structures will become more contrary to their nature. Because there has been comprehensive quality work done on the threat to (or absence of) free speech that these media conglomerates pose, I will not take the time to make a complete analysis here. The point is the complicity of the press in the propaganda wars waged by the government. Without this tool at their disposal, the elite and the government would have no surefire method to promote their agenda. A seminal and topical work regarding the propaganda machine perpetuated by the American mass media is *Manufacturing Consent* by Edward Herman and Noam Chomsky. In this work the authors detail not only the operation of the "propaganda model" as they call it, but also the methods through which this model is implemented and the effect this process has on what sees print and what does not. The startling aspect of this work is not so much their thesis- the American mass media as slave to imperial interests- it is their exhaustive compilation of raw data which verifies the propaganda function of the U.S. mainstream media.

There exists no incentive for these huge companies to dissent from the dominant paradigm. Thus true press nonconformity in America, from both the left and right, is relegated to small, limited-audience media outlets. The affiliation between the government and corporate media interests so seriously threatens the possibility of free speech in America, that talk of freedom of speech becomes a platitude. Offering actual dissenting opinions to the masses has become tantamount to spitting into the wind.

Because these media conglomerates are privately owned, rather than state owned, and because people can generally yell revolutionary slogans from a soapbox without being brutalized by the police, the American media paradigm is an almost self-perpetuating propaganda campaign. The following is a propaganda message the mainstream media delivers with such regularity that most reporters, producers, editors, etc. would hardly recognize it as notable because it is so endemic to their imperial service.

In the January 3, 1999 edition of *The New York Times* there appeared an article about China by Erik Eckholm entitled, "In China, So Many Liberties, So Little Freedom." This article was in no way exceptional from *The New York Times'* typical fare. A rendition of life in China as a land with increasing material opportunities for many and severe oppression dealt out to the few dissidents who resist the tyranny of the Communist Party. Coupled with this analysis was the reputed confusion of Americans who, "...have a hard time understanding how many Chinese can simultaneously appreciate the freedom of the West...and readily dismiss the dissidents as foolish idealists." What this article reinforces is the propaganda campaign that posits the United States as the earthly model of freedom and democracy.

The naiveté of the article becomes rapidly apparent when viewed in the context of the propaganda campaign it serves. For starters, Eckholm focuses mainly on the plight of Chinese dissidents, their harsh treatment by the authorities, and the corresponding general lack of concern from the Chinese public. Eckholm centers on the fact that widespread dissidence in China remains a small concern because, "...the vast majority feel they are finally getting a chance to savor freedom in their personal lives and work, and they want to enjoy the fruits of modern society. The last thing most of them want is upheaval." But the lack of rebellion in China is undoubtedly aided by their governmental media censorship, which mirrors, to a large extent, the role *The New York Times* plays in American society.

If we are to empathize or identify with the plight of the Chinese dissidents, at what point in its history has the corporately-owned and sponsored *New York Times* functioned as a dissenting voice in American culture? Practically never (see Chomsky & Hermann, fair.org, for comprehensive evidence of their pro-power stance). In passing, Eckholm states, "...all news is subtly crafted to serve the interests of the Communists." Yet all one has to do to uncover a similar pattern in the United States is to look at *The New York Times* cover pages during the red scare of the 1920's, the Cold War, or during any American war (covert or overt), to discern the length to which *The New York Times* has been willing to stray from the pro-government, pro-corporate agenda to represent a truly dissident perspective.

If Eckholm's newspaper does not support American dissidents and does support the American regime, is it not logically ludicrous that he would have the American reader identify with Chinese dissidents? Through the use of propaganda that mythologizes America he attempts (either consciously or unconsciously) to engender further support for the power structure which has so greatly benefited *The New York Times* and its advertisers. Thus the capitalist *New York Times'* "news," just like the "subtly crafted news" of the Chinese communists, has the effect of stifling dissent. And the propaganda campaign allows Eckholm, in all sincerity, to conclude his article with the following observation on Chinese dissidents: "Only time will tell whether their countrymen will some day honor them [the Chinese dissident] for their persistence, and their suffering." Unfortunately, his sincerity prevents him from appreciating the irony that he could as well be discussing the plight of the American dissident (Henry David Thoreau, John Brown, Emma Goldman, Eugene Debs, Malcolm X, Martin Luther King, etc.)

Citing this lone example is in no way intended to imply that propaganda campaigns enjoy limited play among the corporate media. The reverse is the case. With the power at their command, these American institutions daily, in every edition of their print, internet, radio and television news programs take the side of the controlling interests who own them, the advertisers that fund them and the power structure that sustains them. There exists no tangible reason (considering the money and power involved) for these corporate entities to act in any other way, or for them to represent the views of dissidents which often stand in direct opposition to everything that has bolstered their success.

INDIVIDUAL ACCOUNTABILITY

With these multifarious control and propaganda structures in place, the questions that remain are those having to do with the individual U.S. citizen's reaction to such stimuli and the effectiveness such propagandized messages and misinformation have on the American public. In other words, are American citizens who live in a society that takes its cues from consumerism, corporations, the elite and materialism, able to effectively form their own opinions within the vacuum of this omnipresent pro-imperial culture?

Eckholm inadvertently touches upon one aspect of this American dilemma in his article about Chinese culture. What confounds Eckholm (and in his opinion, most Americans) about the Chinese is their equating purchasing power with freedom and their inability to observe that "true freedom," as we experience it in the United States, is radically different. In his earnestness Eckholm misses a key point. As noted, the manifestation of historical and contemporary democracy in the United States has been, and remains, negligible. However, depending on their class status, most American citizens have a relative measure of purchasing power. And this consumerism, unlike dissidence, is strongly encouraged not solely by *The New York Times*, but by almost every control structure that exists in the United States. Furthermore, advertisers often use the exercise of one's individuality as a selling angle for their products, as if underscoring that this is the most important way Americans should exercise their freedom.

It would appear then that Eckholm's lament about the hardship of the Chinese dissidents and the failure of seeing through consumerism to the heart of democracy applies equally well in America. One could almost argue that with America's much more powerful corporate presence, this confusion between democracy and materialism is far more advanced in the United States than it is in China.

In their essay entitled, "Mass Communication, Popular Taste, and Organized Social Action," Paul Lazarsfeld and Robert Merton discuss the effects of media on individuals through three different spheres: status conferral, enforcement of social norms and narcotizing dysfunction. In the first sphere the media confer status and legitimacy on people, places and things. In the second sphere the media influences peoples' perceptions by defining what fits within the appropriate bounds of social conduct (shopping) and what does not (dissidence). Finally the narcotizing dysfunction of the mass media creates citizens who are, among other attributes, more passive politically. This essay was written in 1957 and I would argue that due to ever-growing media penetration, Lazarsfeld and Merton's theories are even more relevant regarding the effect that the present-day mass media has on the U.S. population.

Given the prior argument, to what degree does the American retain suzerainty over his or her beliefs? And secondly, to what extent is the average citizen responsible for the suffering caused by the Empire? Because the United States is not a land of extensive freedom nor democracy, expecting the citizenry to act with undiluted free will is optimistic, as there are numerous factors which impact the American mind before it begins to make choices about ideals.

One empty debate between American liberals and conservatives needs to be mentioned here for context. Typically the conservative, calling upon America's myth of individualism, claims that the onus lies with the individual to alter the political landscape. Furthermore, they assert that given American traditions and laws, the tools are present to do so. Liberals argue that the government has the ability to influence lives both positively and negatively, and that structures are in place to defend democracy if our freedoms are threatened.

Neither of these perspectives takes into account the level of historical and contemporary insolvency in American political and social life. These perspectives have functional meaning only within the established, fully corrupted, two-party corporate cabal. When the government and control structures do not have the ability to offer refuge, and the entirety of the political debate serves the rich and powerful, standard liberal and conservative arguments prove largely irrelevant. They function to further the interests of the elite.

Given the artificial belief in America's sanctity, one would expect the average citizen to view dissidence as anathema. And while the effectiveness of this portion of the propaganda effort bears itself out in the still comparatively limited resistance to harmful governmental, military and corporate policies, culpability can still be placed on the individual. Such culpability rests in that part of human nature which has the ability to make a moral or ethical choice. America is a religious country, inhabited by people who are taught and believe in the concepts of human decency, morality and ethical behavior. It is these beliefs that place responsibility on the individual and offers a barometer through which the American registers his or her reaction to the immorality of the Empire. In other words, just as the Empire attempts to encourage disdain for the poor (myth of the individual, materialism, etc.), xenophobia, or any other campaign to misdirect attention from its destructive conduct, a person's discomfort with these actions works as a counterbalance to the machine and places responsibility on the moral individual.

A final consideration for the accountability of the individual citizen resides in the myth of diffused responsibility. In this paradigm, people may become (or are) aware of their suffering, or the suffering cultivated by their nation as a whole, but come to feel that no one can rightly shoulder any blame. This is a deceptive myth, as there are specific individuals (i.e. political, military and corporate leaders) who are blameworthy. And if citizens are able to fuse some responsibility to the leaders of the Empire, it may then be possible for people to recognize the tangible part of the suffering emanating from themselves.

With the condition and actions of the United States Empire as they are, a power beyond temperance, coupled with the underpinnings of myth and propaganda (functions which so dutifully support imperial meanness), the relevance of the citizen to this situation would appear almost nil. Still, there are significant numbers of Americans who resist. The existence of tens if not hundreds of thousands of dissidents in the United States helps indicate two different phenomena. The first is that people can help mollify the negative ramifications of the Empire. It is my belief that all empires go through a process of gradual decline and although one may be able to ameliorate the unneeded anguish intrinsic to the decline, the decline remains inevitable. The theme of lessening the pain caused by the Empire will be addressed again, but it must be emphasized that this angle of reaction carries validity. Secondly, the presence of so many American dissidents, also indicates (as stated by Aldous Huxley in the beginning of this chapter), that propagandists' methods "...are crude and unscientific." There is no other way, beyond the inherent human tendency towards decency and divinity, to describe the existence of these dissidents. American dissidents provide ample evidence that the mythmakers and propagandists cannot have complete control over the outcomes of their efforts. Witness for example, the myth of individualism, which often explodes into virulent anti-authoritarian, anti-government resistance in the form of black power groups, militias, libertarians, anti-globalization protesters and the like. Once again, the propagandists would prefer to use these dissidents as evidence of American democracy, but they cannot have it both ways. Though they would like to possess and dispossess their enemies simultaneously, these peoples' hearts and minds lie beyond the propagandist's realm of influence. If in the future some anthropologist were to analyze the downfall of the U.S. Empire, he or she may look to these dissidents for the germs of its demise.

There remains a large middle class in the United States that -even though it understands the Empire's malice, or partly sees through its propaganda mechanisms- refuses to resist or change its behavior in any consequential way due to its relative wealth and level of satiation. Like the human quality of morality (a universal strength of the species) this type of selfishness is regrettably a universal weakness. Being from this class of people myself and being familiar with its mindset, I would be hard pressed to predict any fundamental change in perspective anytime soon, especially while material comforts (the only real deliverable imperial dividend) persist at an acceptable level.

It is also certainly easier and less unpleasant for this group of people (and many other Americans) to look mistakenly upon the myths and propaganda of the Empire as an innocuous facet of American culture. Since the nation's founding, this class has assisted in strengthening the Empire by promoting the power of the elite. It is a mistake to view propaganda and myth as resembling anything akin to wholesome. As the life of the Empire progresses, the gravity of myth and propaganda does not diminish; they help sustain the Empire by shrouding actual occurrences under alternate guises.

SAVED BY THE BILL?

There are those as well, who steadfastly believe that the Bill of Rights is a panacea for checking the power of the Empire. But "guarantees" such as freedom of the press and free speech are often illusionary, because the real test for the Bill of Rights in a country born of "freedom" and "democracy" is not whether some citizens can cry out heartily against oppression without landing in jail for expressing their beliefs, but rather to what extent has and does the Bill of Rights protect the average individual (foreign or domestic) from the tyranny of the Empire? As our history and recent events have shown, these rights offer small protection. And with a denuded two-party system that has no cause for eradicating policies that coddle the Empire, one must accept that the politicians and militarists are intent on maintaining the current power dynamic for as long as possible.

Tragically, empires have a tendency towards a construct that finds its basis in human frailties and not human ideals. It is then ironic that the powers attributed to empires which indicate their strength, are generally the very same impulses that lead to their downfall (see excessive militarism). This is all part of the American Empire's natural evolution; human weaknesses and frailties played out on a population that is encouraged to nominally participate on the basis of ideals that no empire has ever, or is ever, capable of attaining.

To what do these weaknesses and frailties amount? Should they be pardoned as exponentially exaggerated tendencies? Or do they take on a moral quality whereby human beings, in lusting for temporal power, unleash through the vessel of empire an immoral denunciation of the natural order?

IMPERIALISM AND
THE MYTH OF CIVILIZATION

"...the Romans, whose arrogance it were in vain to shun by obedience and moderation. They are the world's great robbers; when there is no more land left to devastate, they search the seas; they are greedy for money when their enemy is rich, and avid for glory when he is poor; neither East nor West can glut their appetite; they are unique among all peoples in coveting the goods both of rich and of poor with an equal passion of greed. Plunder, butchery, and theft they miscall by the name of "empire," and where they make a solitude, they give it the name of peace."

– QUOTE BY CALGACUS,
the Caledonia Chieftain from Tacitus -1st Century A.D.

"The most remote countries of the ancient world were ransacked to supply the pomp and delicacy of Rome."

– EDWARD GIBBON
The Portable Gibbon: The Decline and Fall of the Roman Empire

"...and that government of the people, by the people, for the people shall not perish from the earth."

– ABRAHAM LINCOLN

"The fortunate and the proud wonder at the insolence of human wretchedness, that it should dare to present itself before them, and with the loathsome aspect of its misery presume to disturb the serenity of their happiness."

– ADAM SMITH

Before exploring the relative morality or immorality of empires, it is first necessary to define the word "empire." There have been large numbers of powerful states throughout human history, but the majority of states have no real claim to this title. The impulse to believe in the unexceptional nature of empires rests in the fact that they have had enormous sway over the course of human events and have presided over the West's cultural legacy. And of course this includes the victor's right of retelling history. Because the social sciences offer few exact solutions or equations for examining social phenomena, my own interpretation of what constitutes an empire will have to suffice, although my parameters should be broad enough to not offend most.

An empire must have the following minimum characteristics: 1.) All empires relative to the time of their existence must not only be large in area, population and internal resources, they must also wield a tremendous amount of external influence. Thus empires must strive to militarily and economically dominate other states and peoples into submission, so that they are assimilated, are enslaved, or, less commonly (they are generally needed economically, see below), eradicated. 2.) Empires must maintain a prevailing military temperament for internal control purposes and for external domination. It follows that these measures are implemented to expand the wealth and power of the ruling class. 3.) The society of an empire is hierarchical in structure with the proceeds from pelf or inequity benefiting a relatively small group of people. 4.) All empires need a large, servile and powerless underclass from which to draw soldiers, products, services, food and taxes for the controlling authority.[i]

Morality as it relates to this system of empires is inexorably linked with dominance, i.e. the will or system of one state forced upon that of others. The key word in the definition is force because it implies the imposition of unwanted rule, and unwanted rule almost always involves violence or the threat of violence. Obviously, a person would only accept this broad definition of morality if they accept the idea that imposing one's will over another, to achieve one's own desires, is immoral.

It is usually the case that states evolve through different stages during their development. Before attaining the status of empire, a state may begin as a tribe of pastoral nomads, a conglomeration of small towns and cities, or (as is often the case) as the subject of another larger state. [ii]Once it has had a turn as an empire, and has been in turn vanquished by another more powerful empire, or fallen due to its own hubris (or both), a state often reverts to its more humble origins, thereby completing an entire lifecycle.

By addressing the root definition and impulses of empires we have to some extent answered several key questions as to their nature, i.e. what are their functions, why are they created and whom do they serve? It is vital to note that in the history of humanity no controlling authority in any empire has put majority interests above its own interests. While this assertion may seem rudimentary, the self-serving behavior of the empires' ruling elites is a cornerstone principle.

As alluded to previously, the sheer influence and power of empires has both skewed and genuinely altered our concept of history and so too our notions of morality. For example, people regularly mistake the measures of the current American Empire as acts of justice (clothed in the political rhetoric of democracy, freedom, etc.), when the immoral acts it commits usually have little to do with ethical standards and more to do with manifestations of power. Empires' potential to do harm is aptly embodied in the ability of imperial authorities to spin propaganda and myth so that they appear to align themselves with positive human impulses.

Prior to discussing in greater depth the inherent immorality of empires, there exists the pertinent issue of their inevitability. If they are inevitable, is there any purpose in offering a critique? Empires are inevitable to the extent that wanton human desires are inevitable. Namely, there are as many examples in human history of kindness, altruism and consideration as there are of wickedness, selfishness and domination. People, at least on an individual level, do have a choice in how they act with others. Barring the rare case of psychosis, the most heinous, hateful people know (if only for a fleeting moment) when their actions clash with their spiritual beliefs, and the same can be said for the rulers of empires. This paradigm hints at an alternate reality in which humans appropriately recognize empires as profane and allows for a reasoned critique against their immorality and their inevitability.

Beneficiaries of the American Empire would have people believe, that even if all of these aspects of historical empires exist, they are certainly not true in the case of the United States. They would argue that this nation was uniquely founded on the lofty principles of freedom and democracy (and the market) in order that it may avoid the moral bankruptcy of previous empires.

The pressing reason for judging empires through a window of morality is that without accounting for this defining element, there is no way to accurately comprehend their purpose, or correspondingly, to understand the historical context of the American Empire. Empires, under the guidance of their leaders, always act in a manner that attempts to insure the leaders' control over their subjects at any cost. The materialization of this control effort takes place both inside and outside the physical borders of the empire. Let us focus on the control structures, societal hierarchy, the underclass and the militarism necessary for maintaining these regimes.

Before delving into a selection of historical empires, a key point must be made: in no way do I intend to forward the idea that these empires are identical to each other in every manner. The scope of history remains far too wide for a minute breakdown of human interactions at every different level of these societies. Nor is an all-encompassing consideration of the relationship between these empires, their peoples and all outside peoples with whom they came into contact, realistic. What I am arguing is that while these empires may have differed widely in some aspects of their being, there are discernable macro-concepts linking them all together. These traits constitute their prevailing nature and form a framework wherein the actions of imperial rulers and societies become transparent.

EGYPT

For people interested in Egyptian history, the one aspect of the society that clearly stands out above all else is its social hierarchy. Because societal stratification (with a ruling few acting as a control structure over a massive underclass) is the bedrock of modern western empires it is appropriate to look at this reality within Egyptian society. According to Egyptian historian Barbara Watterson, distinct class divisions were present in Egypt as early as 3000b.c. (Watterson 1997, p. 37 & 39). The Egyptian political system which evolved through the centuries had certain essential qualities, that, when the state was functioning on a normal level, were remarkably consistent. The Egyptian pharaoh occupied the top of the social hierarchy and claimed (demanded) to be viewed as a god. While more recent empires also used religion as a tangible power mechanism, the Egyptian version of this technique lacked any subtlety. Myths surrounding the Egyptian god-kings also played a role in their succession, and thus often facilitated the handing of power from one king to another through familial bloodlines (Clark 1982, p. 660).

Like any society based on a hierarchical model, Egyptian empires had to possess a subordinate, elite class willing to promote and help operate the divine kingdom. According to The Cambridge History of Africa, one of the marked accomplishments of Early Dynastic Egyptian society was the development of an elite class tradition (Clark 1982, p. 546). It is hard to gauge whether or not this circumstance of Egyptian culture benefited the masses of peasants ruled over by the pharaohs and the elite. The benefits derived (at least in terms of material wealth by the kings and their adjutants) is evident to this day in the opulence of their symbolic pyramidal graves, built by the masses in honor of the pharaohs.

That the pharaohs and the elite depended on the labor (sometimes slave), military enlistment and taxation levied upon the proletariats, remains, like the obvious social hierarchy of the Egyptian empires, relatively unambiguous. Because detailed historical information about the specifics of Egyptian culture is at best a little sketchy, determination of particulars proves a difficult task. Clearly though, the Egyptians' leaders had a keen affinity for militarism, materialism and were fixated on wealth. The records kept on financial and military matters were written inside the tombs themselves and were evidence of this worship. It is through these artifacts that we are able to perceive that the ruling class and pharaohs exacted a severe toll from their own people and the people they conquered.

Considering the antiquity of the Egyptian empires, one would hardly expect them to have developed an extensive bureaucracy for the collection of taxes. The system was, however, mature and sophisticated (Watterson 1997, p. 45). This demonstrates one of the potent, illuminating laws driving the ruling structure of Egypt (and of all empires): always contribute to one's own appetite, to excess when possible. And so as the Egyptian authority's power gradually increased and became centralized throughout the 4th Dynasty of the Old Kingdom, the building of the elaborate pyramids we now so strongly associate with the empire, truly flourished.

Instead of glorifying and sitting in wonderment of the amazing building prowess and abilities required to fabricate these monuments (as the mainstream historians of Western civilization tell us that we should) -let us ponder how it would be possible for a small band of rulers to have these temples constructed in self-glorification with no mechanical contrivances. The simple answer is the toil of the masses. While it is not a mystery to most modern people that the poor and slaves assembled the pyramids, this revelatory fact is not generally emphasized by mainstream historians. Turning the focus upon the manufacturers, rather than marveling at the beauty of these creations, allows for a more lucid understanding of the connection between ancient Egypt and present-day empires, and the pyramids appear justly for what they are; examples of excessive power, created at the behest of avaricious rulers.

Next we must consider Egypt's culture of militarism. To truly qualify as a standard bearer for empires (and as an empire in its own right), Egypt would need armed control mechanisms to accompany its social hierarchy. During the 4th Dynasty (2613-2589 B.C.) under the pharaoh Sneferu, there are written records of wars fought abroad in Nubia and Libya, with further indications of booty taken in the form of prisoners and cattle (Watterson 1997, p. 49 & 51). For Pharaohs to guarantee personal benefits from these conflicts, the creation of a military was essential. Thus an influential military class developed with the pharaohs' passing on gifts, slaves, land and other booty to the armed forces for their successes (Watterson 1997, p. 125 & Eisenstadt 1967, p. 36).

The era of the New Kingdom saw rapid military advancement to the point that the pharaohs came close to uniting all of the urban centers of the Middle East under common Egyptian rule (Curtin et. al 1978, p. 50). As one example, the decentralized Palestinians and their lands on the Sinai Peninsula were relatively easy conquests, though not without adverse effects on Palestinian culture (Clark 1982, p. 727). Aside from providing men for the military and taxes in the form of agricultural surpluses, the bulk of the Egyptian populace enjoyed little in the way of political authority (Clark 1982, p. 838-839 & 841 & Eisenstadt 1967, p. 46-47). Thus the ultimate consequence of these excursions was to consolidate ruling class wealth, to heighten the pharaohs' power, and to help Egypt develop a near monopoly on trade in the region; all of which led to the establishment of a permanent professional army with close ties to the god-kings (Clark 1982, p. 853).

Although this account of Egypt is far from encyclopedic, it does reveal some basic truths about this society that are fairly well supported even by mainstream texts like The Cambridge History of Africa. With the pattern of internal and external abuses exercised by the rulers of ancient Egypt now established, we must consider similar immoral behavior of subsequent western empires.

ROME

No study of imperial immorality would be complete without a quick glimpse at the Roman Empire, for it is here that the terrible vision of humanity prescribed by the rulers of empires comes into full fruition. The influence of the Romans was so great that their legacy defined the corrupt version of civilization posited upon the world's citizens by today's mythmakers, always ready to define the debate by ignoring the bloodshed and decadence in favor of tales regaling governmental systems, valorous military campaigns and technological advancements. This brief discussion will focus instead on Roman indiscretions, with close attention to attributes which testify to imperial rapaciousness and immorality.

Roman rulers shared the Egyptian rulers' affinity for self-indulgence, but the Roman Empire was a more technically evolved hierarchy than that of Egypt. Their ingenuity in creating a militaristic empire has fascinated historians for centuries. Remarking upon Roman grandeur serves, like the adoration of the pyramids, to perpetuate the mythology. Tales of this sort make wonderful children's stories, full of heroes, geniuses and conquerors, but what sort of reality did the Roman majority experience? If we are to judge the Roman Empire's immorality, then we must look at the instruments which enabled generations of ruling class Romans to enslave hundreds of thousands, to internally and externally (through rampant militarism) subjugate millions more, and to savagely conquer lands that ultimately included territory on three continents.

This description is not an effort to say that every mainstream text on Roman history, of the thousands produced, universally offer some kind of pat regurgitation of facts serving only to promote the glories of Western civilization. However, many historians are uncomfortable forming ethical opinions, particularly when considering an empire with the breadth and depth of influence wielded by the Romans. By not forming such opinions, and through glorifying Roman behavior, many historians have tacitly supported what took place. Of course one can take the information they provide and arrive at profound moral conclusions. But to understand the truth behind the Romans' actions, and their influence on the empires that followed, these excesses must be considered.

Prior to digesting the immoral actions of the Roman rulers, I will quickly address two anticipated arguments in defense of the Empire. The first has to do with citizenship. Many see Roman citizenship as one harbinger of modern "liberal democracies." It should be made clear that this citizenship was a legal right and did not ensure the citizens a voice in how they were governed (Clarke 1994, p. 14). The granting of citizenship to people conquered through Roman militarism, helped to sustain, expand and foster the Empire (Heichelheim 1970, p.266 & Barker, et al. 1954, p.236). The second protest may be an objection to applying 20th century moral standards to antiquarian societies. For an abbreviated rebuttal of this reasoning, a glance at the 1st century A.D. quote heading up this chapter proves that at least some people from the that era viewed Roman behavior with similar criteria to what will be used here.

A revealing area in which to start this exploration is the Roman labor system, specifically with regards to slave labor. To what extent did this Empire, credited in part with the emancipation of the Western mentality from the cloistered mindset of the ancient world, depend upon slavery for its elevation? Part of the dilemma, as with any study of earlier societies, has to do with the problem of ascertaining exact statistics from centuries-old sources. At the risk of seeming arbitrary, and after determining that the majority of Roman historians view slavery as playing a major role in that society, I will follow the numbers of one source, more to provide clarity on the importance of slavery to the Romans than to enter into a debate as to precise figures which are admittedly indeterminate. I treat the following numbers as reasonable estimates.

Based on John Madden's analysis, the percentage of slaves in the city of Rome during the 1st century A.D. (i.e. the initial years of the Empire, following the Roman Republic) was roughly a third of the total population (Madden 1996, p.1). His assessment of the percentage of slaves within present day Italy during this same period mirrors that of the city, with slaves representing about 1/3 of the population (Ibid, p.1). For the Empire (which at its height encompassed a geographical area that stretched from England to present-day Iran.) as a whole he surmises that 16.6% to 20% of the population was enslaved (Ibid, p. 2). With numbers approaching these levels, this snapshot of Roman society reveals a culture heavily reliant upon the forced labor of an extensive underclass for internal and external operations.

As with all societies, certain components depend on each other for survival and support. This happens to be the situation with the Roman military and Rome's dependence on slave labor. As is the case with the calculation of the literal number of slaves in the Empire, no historian has been able to unilaterally determine every contributing source of slaves, although it is clear that thousands were forced into service through military plunder.

Militarism went much further than acting as an avenue to gather cheap labor. It permeated every level of society, and thus, to a great degree, helped define the Roman character. Augustus, the Emperor credited with elevating the imperial system, was a military ruler. This appraisal is a view commonly held by historians (Barker, et al. 1954, p. 222) and by Augustus' chroniclers (Barker 1956, p. 224-229). According to Augustus himself (or more likely, his ghost writer) from inscriptions found in Ankara, Turkey his prestige was very much derived from his success as a military commander, which is obvious from the repeated references to battles and the forced indenture of various foreign peoples (Ibid., p. 224-229). Augustus' militaristic outlook and dependence on the military for power were models that would shape the future course of the Empire and its emperors. Interesting to note is the desire of the Roman rulers to foment the worship of militarism, and to have as their leader someone who also acted as the army's Commander-in-Chief.

The promotion of a militaristic bias among the society as a whole was a triumph of the ruling class. Once again, it is hard to ascertain the precise number of individuals in the armed forces. What we are able to tell, from the abundance (and geographical disparity) of lands conquered, and from the frequency of military actions, is the military's importance to the functioning of everyday Roman society. The Roman legions, "...were almost constantly involved in conquering new territory, punishing an upstart neighbor, or suppressing a native rebellion..." (Cameron 1989, p. 39). And it was primarily the Italian peasantry that contributed, at least in the nascent stages of Roman power, to the realization of these military exploits (McNeill 1963, p. 314). There should be little question that the emperors' own desires were very directly realized by the military. On the one hand, the military provided for their protection. According to one account, Augustus and his successors had up to 9,000 privileged Praetorian guards, stationed throughout Italy, serving as official bodyguards (Barker, et al. 1954, p. 223). On the other hand it helped them add to their personal fortunes

(Heichelheim 1970, p.272). The Empire's treasury, however, suffered larger blows than losses from greedy emperors, with the biggest part of the state budget going to the army and the navy (Ibid., p, 273). Accordingly, Edward Gibbon suggests that people's fear of the military gave the emperors formidable clout and that Roman leaders preserved "peace" through a constant readiness for war (Gibbon 1952, p. 35).

Additional evidence of the army's predominant role in Roman society can be seen in the substantial number of emperors who were either appointed by the military or were generals who became emperors. From the reign of Augustus (27b.c.-14a.d.) through the reign of Diocletian (284a.d.-305a.d.) - the emperor responsible for splitting the Empire into eastern and western sections- almost a third of the Emperors were appointed by the military or were military commanders.

Allowing for my own standards of imperial immorality, such excessive militarism and extensive slavery still do not provide a complete indictment. For an empire to achieve a full state of wantonness, its social makeup must be taken into account. The Roman leaders sacked, occupied, and enslaved foreign lands and peoples, but if they had otherwise contributed to creating an equitable, non-hierarchical, libertarian society, then an accusation of immorality would be partly unjust. Far from failing this last test, though, the societal construction of the Roman Empire provides the evidence of its native immorality.

In studies concerning the age of Empire, one encounters repeated references to societal iniquities, even as these same texts emphasize the world's debt to Roman culture. The following are a few examples of fantastic Roman transgressions provided by mainstream historians and economists. When there exists in the text a corresponding, adjacent accolade of Roman behavior, it is included.

In his work *An Ancient Economic History*, Fritz Heichelheim states, "The Government machine, so lacking in Republican times, developed under Augustus, starting from ancient Roman traditions, to show a fruitful promise, while its officials formed the class which upheld the traditions of the

Empire...the tax restrictions and the settlement policies introduced by Caesar, Augustus and the numerous Emperors of the first and 2nd centuries A.D. were not able to prevent an increasing loss in independence on the part of the peasants." Agricultural peasants represented the overwhelming majority of Romans and it was on these masses that taxes were levied by the state. From these coffers the ruling class derived their essential monies (Eisenstadt 1967, p. 72).

Another example of Roman societal dysfunction presented within a similarly schizophrenic framework occurs in The European Inheritance Volume I by Ernest Barker, et al. Referring to the Emperor Trajan, they comment: "His legislation was marked by humanity and care for the young; he carried out great public works and improved military communications" (Barker et. al. 1954, p. 232). However, a quote on the same page relates: "Trajan broke up the Dacian people, filled the land with new settlers, and brought home many captives and a vast treasure in gold." Their general summation of Trajan's rule is: "Certainly prosperity was widespread and the empire seemed to be running like a well-oiled machine (Ibid. p. 235)." And, that: "...it meant something to fill your part, however small, in the enormous prestige of the empire, based firmly on the ruling ideas of the 'immense majesty of the Roman people' and the Roman Peace (Ibid., p. 235)." A less fawning assessment on Roman society comes from Rondo Cameron:

> "Most productive work was done either by slaves or by servile peasants whose status differed little from that of slaves. Even if they had had an opportunity to improve technology, they would have reaped few if any benefits, either in terms of higher incomes or reduced labor. Members of the small privileged classes devoted themselves to war, government, the cultivation of the fine arts and sciences, and conspicuous consumption. [and] ...labor carried the stigma of menial status (Cameron 1989, p. 43)."

If one looks at such seemingly incongruous conclusions through the myth of constant Western "progress," then these historical presentations become less incomprehensible. Like the American myth of democracy, if Rome were not looked upon as an admirable cultural and societal mentor, our current institutions would have much less legitimacy. Or perhaps historians are more afflicted by the typical social science syndrome whereby ethical and moral judgements are to be avoided at all costs. Still, by lauding the Romans' behavior and more importantly by overlooking the parallels between their brutality and ours, a judgement is made, and the truth is buried.

GREAT BRITAIN

A few thoughts on British Empire are material to the current argument because of the obvious connection to the United States, and also because Britain can serve as a bridge between ancient Rome and modernity.

Similar to the Egyptians and the Romans, the British Empire enjoyed a fairly lengthy reign as a premier arbiter of world politics. Depending on when one believes it truly began, the British Empire enjoyed at least 400 years of global significance. The British were unlike their Egyptian and Roman forbears in a few pertinent ways. What sets them apart from Egypt and Rome is the global scale of their power and the use of their worldwide subjects as tools for the expansion of a pseudo-capitalist economy. This global perspective was also unique in that, other than in the regional colonies of Great Britain, i.e., Ireland, Wales and Scotland, their influence was more strongly felt outside of their immediate realm. This is not to say that their power did not affect relations with their Continental neighbors, nor that wrangling over colonies did not play a significant role in European affairs, but merely that British ascendancy was experienced more acutely by Native Americans and the Indian Subcontinent than by the French or the Germans. Physically separated from the rest of Europe, the British, after subjugating the peoples on their islands, turned their gaze outward. They used their military to establish markets which would support the hierarchy and extravagance of the monarchy and the nobility.

The reason the term pseudo-capitalism is used here has to do with the particular brand of capitalism developed by the British Empire. This form of economics owes much more to the power politics of empires than it does to any love of free-markets. Myths surrounding the British system of "free-market capital-ism" are so powerful that they persist to this day in first world interactions with the developing world. The notion that an economic relationship between a mil-itarily dominant state and an undeveloped state can be anything like "free," or that the ruling classes in the British Empire -or in modern day "capitalist" soci-eties for that matter- did not derive overwhelming protection and governmental benefits above and beyond the obvious military assistance, is absurd.

According to Anthony Pagden, the British authorities learned from colo-nial practices in America that it was less expensive to tap into cheap foreign labor than to encourage settlements which might eventually gain enough wealth to turn against the mother country (Pagden 1995, p. 7-8).[iii] Thus, to a large degree, the British Empire retooled itself along these lines and established a colonial eco-nomic regime spreading from the Caribbean to southern Asia. The primary effects of these activities were the virtual enslavement of millions, a massive buildup in the wealth of Britain's upper classes and an even further expansion of and justification for its military.

As early as the first part of the 18th century, citizens of European descent in the British West Indies numbered 30,000, while 120,000 people were of indige-nous or African descent (Parry 1971, p. 47). This disparity created a situation whereby the white representatives of British imperialism were effectively a garri-son among slaves (Ibid., p. 47). In 1833 the Empire abolished slavery and the effects on the plantation class in the West Indies were devastating (Judd 1996, p. 84). From 1828 to 1850, Jamaica's worldwide share of sugar production fell from 15% to 2.5% (Ibid., p. 85).[iv]

Conditions in India during the era of British control were equally grim. More elaborate control structures were established on the Subcontinent than in the Caribbean. The British authorities instituted a land tax on the peasants which went to pay for a large portion of the occupying administrative and mil-itary forces (Thompson 1999, p. 108). Indians paid 10 million pounds a year in taxes and revenue to the British, which was over and above the multi-million pound balance of trade in England's favor (Judd 1996, p. 77). By the end of the 19th century, 40% of India's revenue was spent to pay for the Indian military (Ibid., p. 77). In other brilliant, albeit malicious machinations, the military was comprised partially of Indians, and the British employed former members of the Indian ruling class as a buffer between themselves and the masses (Thompson 1999, p. 108-109). [v]

Considering the aforementioned examples of Britain's imperial behavior, let's take a look at the actual reality behind their "capitalist" system. As mentioned previously, the myth of British capitalism, even in the face of strong evidence to the contrary, reveals itself in many of our modern day institutions of globalization. The fundamental falsities of this myth posit that trading partners are equal and willing participants, with the benefits of trade going impartially to both parties. Other aspects of this myth revolve around the advantages presented by this "capitalism" to all classes of society, which we will explore in a moment when we weigh the costs and benefits to British society.

In this admittedly brief analysis of Great Britain's external behavior, it is clear that it fills my criteria relating to imperial meanness. But what of its internal society? Did the British authorities' rapaciousness and oppression abroad lead to a glorified society at home, thereby eliminating it from contention as a true empire, and thus, to the detriment of this argument, making the English (at least internally) an exception to the standards of imperial immorality? There are those who promote this as the case, citing the British tradition of charity towards the poor and the creation of the first modern welfare state. [vi] There are centuries-old debates among British scholars, philosophers and politicians regarding the appropriate relationship between the state and its impoverished citizens. However, I would venture to say that many modern pro-capitalist thinkers have a vested interest in a positive portrayal of imperial British society, which is very much a model for the predominant present-day economic edifice.

In the final undertaking, the dream of any real societal equality during the reign of the British Empire must be seen for what it is: an illusion. What we find instead is a society that provides a model for the ruling-elite version of governance. And more relevantly, affords a solid example of an immoral imperial system.

As stated, there has been and still is a rather fierce debate surrounding the level of historical inequality in Great Britain. On the one hand are capital apologists who argue that although industrialization caused some inequality, the overall effect on the Empire's internal subjects was positive (Williamson 1985). And there are those like Marx who reasoned that the fundamental iniquity of British society was merely a stepping-stone to a more enlightened worker-led civilization.

While some segments of the British population may have been able to purchase more goods as factory workers than as farm laborers through industrialization (spurred by the Empire's global hegemony), little changed in the primal construction of British society.[vii] Available statistics of Great Britain's societal makeup during this period of imperial dominance reveal a staunchly hierarchical society. The capitalists' theories only work if one considers larger questions of inequality off limits, i.e. that there have always been winners and losers in this world and therefore questions of fairness must be seen as moot. But, when we observe Great Britain through the lens of empires' immorality, there is evidence enough to discredit the pro-capitalist rendition of reality.

One brief explanatory note needs to be made before looking at statistics whose accuracy, due to historical limitations, may be subject to slight variations. The observation relates to overwhelming evidence and requires a touch of common sense. Anyone who reads mainstream texts about the British Empire will find it nearly impossible to avoid repeated references to British royalty, leaders of parliament and large owners of capital. The reasons for this are twofold. First, any credible historian understands the nature of British hierarchy and that it was these people who reaped, by far, the greatest benefit from the Empire's actions. Secondly, we are treated to a top-down rendition of British history because it reflects precisely these individuals' power to literally and figuratively dictate the course of history.

Therefore, with eyes slightly opened, we can begin to appreciate British iniquity, flawed statistics or no.

According to a late 17th century statistical breakdown of British society, more than two million citizens out of a population of five and a half million were found to be poor or paupers (Himmelfarb 1983, p. 27). Using a pro-capitalist text we find that from 1688 to 1801-3 the richest 35% of the population gained larger shares of income at the expense of the middle and lower classes, and that between 1801 to 1867 the top 5% to 10% of the population profited acutely (Williamson 1985, p. 67). In his book titled *Wealth and Inequality in Britain*, W.D. Rubinstein states that until very recently the British working class (estimated near 75% of the total population) was without property and nearly impoverished (Rubinstein 1986, p. 111-112). Between 1830 and 1914 (during an industrial boom) the range of incomes around the average did not lessen, with the rich remaining much richer than the average and the poor much poorer (Floud 1997, p. 15). In 1914 up to a third of British citizens could not afford food sufficient to maintain yearlong health (Ibid., p. 15). Coincidentally, in 1914 the British Empire also controlled 25% of the world's land mass (Ibid., p. 168). All of these figures attest to what common sense indicates; the British Empire, like the empires before it, thrived on a horribly unequal society.

It is widespread among historians to laud the British for their contribution to modern "democracy." As with the previously discussed American Bill of Rights, there exists a tremendous gulf between historical fantasy and reality. Much of this mythology finds sustenance in the right of British citizens to vote. Following the Reform act of 1832, representation in Parliament was reapportioned to more closely represent the changing industrial population centers (Everett 1987, p. 1). This act also controversially (further revealing the state of British "democracy") granted suffrage to males with households worth ten pounds, or about 1 in 5 men (Ibid., p. 1). In fact, it would not be until 1928 (after various subsequent "controversial" acts), in the waning years of the Empire, that all adult men and women were given the right to vote (Ibid., p. 1).

One may conclude that this sort of progression towards our present-day under-standing of representative democracy fills the necessary requirements for Britain to be seen as a model for modern democracies. Or, using the historical record as a guide, one can observe Great Britain for what it was: a bastion of tyranny that practiced upon its internal and external subjects the oppression and domination characteristic of an anti-democratic, imperial society.

WASHINGTON D.C.:
SEAT OF THE AMERICAN EMPIRE

Washington D.C., as with the capital cities of the Roman and British empires, is a potent symbol of the society it represents. Both Rome and London were great seats of power. They were also rife with the destitute and were plagued with unprecedented levels of inequality both in terms of wealth and class. Thus it seems only fitting, at least initially, to look at the current American Empire through the workings of its capital.

A look at Washington's society provides two lasting impressions. The first is that the majority of the city's black citizens live in a world unrelated to that of its white inhabitants and secondly, that improvements of the city's deplorable social conditions appear to be beyond the scope of the government's concern. Both of these factors heavily contribute to Washington's symbolic potency and durable status as the most beleaguered capital of the modern industrialized world.

According to recent United States' census bureau information, Washington D.C., when compared with states, ranked first in the entire country in rates of violent crime and overall crime (2003 FBI -Uniform Crime Report). In 2003 there were 1,608 incidents of violent crime per 100,000 people in D.C., almost four times the national average of 475 inci-dents per 100,000 (U.S. Census Bureau). In 1999, D.C. was second only to Detroit in the rate of violent crime for a major U.S. city (1999 FBI - Crime in the United States). These statistics attest to what many Americans and all of the federal policy-makers already know; Washington D.C. is perennially one of the most violent and troubled communities in the United States.

The nature of Washington's societal breakdown is truly revealed in its income distribution, education, and rates of incarceration figures. In 2000, the average per capita income of a white resident of Washington D.C. was $52,552 (U.S. Census Bureau). In that same year an average black resident made $17,734 (Ibid.). The difference between the two figures is staggering, with whites earning almost three times as much as blacks. According to the U.S. Census Bureau, the number of black D.C. residents in 1990 over the age of 25 without a high school diploma was 95,006, compared to 9,136 for white residents (Ibid.). The incarceration rates for the two races are equally disturbing. In 2000 the rates of incarceration were 46 per 100,000 whites to 768 per 100,000 blacks (Ibid.). Although a larger percentage of Washington's citizens are black (176,101 whites to 343,312 blacks according to 2000 U.S. Census Data), it is hard to ignore imbalances of this magnitude.

The status of race relations between blacks and whites in D.C. is symbolic of race relations nationwide. While there are certainly wealthy and middle class black citizens in the United States, just as there are disenfranchised, impoverished whites, the general conditions of the two races differ vastly. On average white Americans live longer, are less likely to be incarcerated, have a lower percentage of infant deaths, are wealthier and have more educational opportunities (U.S. Census Bureau, CDC, NCHS and The Sentencing Project).viii Although it would be almost impossible to ascertain whether individuals or the authorities deserve more credit for fomenting racism, there is no question that the government is, at the very least, tacitly complicit.

As to why there are such dramatic, racially-determined differences between the lives of white and black citizens in D.C., the answers are numerous and have been addressed in great depth by many scholars. I do think however, that with regards to race issues in the United States, the aforementioned question may not be as applicable as an alternate question, i.e., what do these present, perennial conditions tell us about American society?

Defects of this size would never be accepted by a government in a genuinely (or even nominally) democratic society. A government and power structure so removed from notions of decency, willing to ignore and minimize the suffering of certain segments of its citizenry, indicates that undemocratic behavior is a fundamental trait of its character.

While black people bear the vast burden of suffering in Washington, there are other statistics which provide evidence of a generalized societal breakdown. In 2000 31.1% of the of the city's populace under the age of 18 were living in poverty (U.S. Census Bureau). The number that same year for families with children under the age of 5 living in poverty was 29.5% (Ibid.).[ix] In 2003 the infant death rate was 10 per 1000 births compared with the national average of 6.9 per 1,000 (Associated Press, 10/21/05). And while this is an improvement over 1995's rate of 16.2 per 1,000 births, two of the poorest wards were still reporting mortality rates more than double the national average in 2003 (Ibid.).

While it is possible to find ample historical evidence of people blind to the nature of their rulers, rarer are the instances of rulers blind to the nature of their subjects. It is of utmost importance for the federal authorities to keep citizens' concerns about inequality in check. In America there are typically several different governmental and corporate bodies which hold sway over an individual's life, thus it may seem shortsighted to lay the blame of Washington's societal breakdown on the federal authorities alone, unless, of course, they are the categorically accountable power. Therefore, the logical question is who are the ultimate, direct and accountable policy decision-makers in the Capital's government? The sheer size of the United States can make the pursuit of accountability in ruling authorities almost fruitless. And often, due to the enormous power and influence the rulers hold, they are able to obfuscate the truth.

WHO GOVERNS WASHINGTON D.C.?

Washington D.C.'s form of government makes it unique and thus a worthy case study for accountability. Unlike other state governments in America, D.C.

is directly controlled by the federal government of the United States. There are local authorities, but all final decisions and cash flow are (and have been) dictated by Congress and the President. In terms of governmental responsibility, if one looks to assign culpability for the city's failure, there are few legitimate options beyond the federal authorities.

According to a lawsuit filed by a group of D.C. citizens against the federal authorities, for (among other grievances) violating their constitutional rights of self-representation, the federal government terminated the state citizenship rights of Washington's constituents in 1801 (Adams et. al. vs. Clinton et. al.). By 1895, the U.S. Congress placed the full authority to govern the District of Columbia in the hands of a three-person commission appointed by the President (Adams et. al. vs. Clinton et. al.). In 1973 Congress created what was called the "Home-Rule government" (which consisted of a locally elected mayor and city council), a name that was a misnomer as Congress retained veto power over most important issues and decisions (Adams et. al. vs. Clinton et. al.). After more than twenty years of "home-rule," Congress once again exerted its control over the Capital's affairs by establishing the Financial Responsibility and Management Assistance Authority whose charge was to supervise the "home-rule government" (Adams et. al. vs. Clinton et. al.). Finally, in 1997 Congress terminated the last vestiges of local government autonomy as control was turned over to the Financial Responsibility and Management Assistance Authority whose five members are selected by the President (Adams et. al. vs. Clinton et. al.).

The preceding information is instructive as it answers unequivocally the question of historical and contemporary governmental authority in Washington D.C. For over two hundred years the U.S. Government has been directly in charge of the city and its inhabitants. Since we have already discussed the current state of affairs in D.C. and have unveiled the federal government as the ruling entity, some unnerving conclusions become inescapable. But before drawing these conclusions and considering their implications, a few more issues need consideration.

THE ROLE OF THE STATE

A predictable counter-argument to the forgoing details lay in one's perception of the government's role in society. Although the classic Republican versus Democrat argument is a bit of a distraction from the heart of the matter, the parties' hold on American political life is so pervasive that to not mention it at all would be unmindful. Without straying too far from the topic at hand, here is a brief synopsis of the ruling parties' rhetoric around the government's societal role. Republican rhetoric revolves around a professed adherence to limiting government involvement in citizens' personal and business lives (although this perspective is not shared by the party's totalitarian wing), while Democratic rhetoric focuses on the government helping people improve their lot via programs, services, etc. This is just a thumb-nail sketch of the parties' positions; the true nature of these parties' purpose and their relationship with each other will be discussed later.

In societies led by fascists or dictators, the state is merely a control mechanism created to serve the interests of those in power. In democratic (or nominally-democratic) societies, the role of the state is ostensibly less nefarious. While control mechanisms are still tangible, there are also certain liberties and freedoms which cannot, by force of law or mutual agreement, be violated by those in positions of authority.[x] People should also be able to reasonably expect a representative government to serve their interests in some way, especially if that government derives its existence through constituent taxation. In theory, a government set up to serve the people (as opposed to the self-interest of its authorities) is a determinant which distinguishes representative democracies from fascism and dictatorships.

I have made this definition as broad as possible to try to avoid the usual debate around the state's role in this form of government. Reducing representative democracy to such fundamentals is not an effort in simplification. I am merely attempting to define a baseline of privilege due a citizen living in such a society in order to determine if the average Washingtonian enjoys these rights.

There is one other political theory that Republicans (and some Democrats) invoke which tends to whitewash calls of governmental impropriety and serves to shield the government from accountability. This doctrine preaches that the individual's primacy for his or her own well-being takes precedence over any state responsibility. Therefore, while it appears obvious in the case of Washington D.C. that the federal government had no entity to blame but itself, many government officials and citizens alike tend to put the blame on the masses.

The American belief in individualism bears the fruit of other similar myths, namely that of diverting attention from the truly responsible entities. Notwithstanding situations such as businesses receiving billions in annual tax breaks, or the fact that if the U.S. government were half its current size, it would continue to be heavily enmeshed in individuals' lives, the ultimate theoretical flaw for those who blame the individual is that they ignore the incredibly pertinent fact that the disenfranchised were disenfranchised by the very system that the individualists refuse to prosecute. In other words, there are many pre-existing systems into which the average poor, black child in Washington D.C. is born and over which they have no control, i.e. racism, violence, poverty, incarceration, segregation, educational inequality, etc. For centuries, placing blame on the victims has been a tool used by the powerful to squelch dissent. And for the United States politician a positive result of this practice has been that large numbers of the populace have come to believe it as truth. In reality, genuine individual accountability is anathema to most American rulers for it is only legitimate in political systems devoid of centralized authority and predicated on authentic freedom. What would these same leaders who laud freedom do with no subjects to control?

There is one last question with respect to governmental authority and responsibility, and that is the question of money. A representative government's ability to serve its populace is directly related to the amount of money it collects in taxes and other fees. Although the taxation rates in the United States are not as high as those in more socialistic industrialized nations, the United States is the richest country on earth. Logically a wealthy country should be more equipped to serve its constituents than a poor one.

Allowing that one of the established minimum factors which qualify a nation as a representative democracy is the duty of the government to serve its people -as opposed to the interests of its rulers- and given that the United States has more financial resources than any other nation, and that the government of the United States has directly controlled Washington D.C. for over two hundred years, one would have to assume that the citizens of the nation's capital live in a thriving, healthy society. However, we know that the majority of Washington's residents live in a city with rampant social apartheid. A disparity of this dimension, which seemingly defies even the most broadly drawn parameters of what a representative democracy should offer its citizens, supports the idea that other conclusions can be drawn from the information at hand.

"OF, BY AND FOR THE PEOPLE"

An interesting way to frame these incongruities is to consider the present-day reality of Washington D.C. as it relates to Lincoln's famous line from his Gettysburg address, "...that government of the people, by the people, for the people shall not perish from the earth." The strength of Lincoln's words rests in their proximity to the rudiments of democracy and is the reason they are frequently recalled. The words, within their simple parameters, eloquently and succinctly affirm democracy's tenets.

If the United States government were in fact a government "of, by or for the people," what disenfranchised person in D.C. would ever choose a government such as this? Who but the most self-immolating individual would chose a government that spends trillions of dollars (Schwartz, 1998) on nuclear weapons and does so little to alleviate the suffering of its capital's citizens? (The indifference persists in 2006, with President Bush's budget proposal calling for a 6.9% increase in defense spending to 439 billion -not including his wars in Afghanistan and Iraq, with corresponding calls for killing or cutting 141 social programs amounting to a savings of 15 billion.) There are two basic answers to these questions. First, because Washington D.C. is dominated by the federal government, the residents of Washington D.C. elect local leaders who have no power.[xi] The second, and more ominous conclusion is that the government of the United States is not a government "of, for or by the people."

One might argue that the government is a government "for the people," meaning that even though it is negligibly responsible to the will of the people, it is moral enough to put the well-being of its constituents before concerns of business and power. Regrettably, this too is not a reality. Without belaboring a point which has been touched on before and will be addressed again in later chapters, the United States government spends billions a year on militarism, security organizations (CIA, FBI, NSA, etc.) and prisons, and billions more on tax relief for billion dollar corporations, factors which do not indicate a government with an intact democratic compass. The foregoing expenditures are so gratuitous, that even if the United States were a country with limited social needs, such spending would testify to inveterate governmental malfeasance. In helping to care for the majority of its citizens (not the minority who benefit greatly from its policies), the United States fares no better than any of the other historical empires that preceded it. In relation to Lincoln's idea of democracy, the citizens of Washington D.C. are afforded little in the way of the rights which he perceived to be paramount to a democratic nation, yet the myth surrounding his words perseveres unabated in the face of overwhelming evidence to the contrary.

Delving into the motives of the policy-makers may help reveal whether the authorities are unwilling or simply unable to serve and govern the people. The notion that the government is unwilling to serve or govern the people of Washington D.C. (and by extension the people of the United States) is unnerving but difficult to refute. The riches of the government, juxtaposed with irrefutable public suffering, leads to this summation. The implication of this summary is that the government is a bereft institution in so far as serving the people, and more tellingly, does serve the interests of a ruling elite, the military and corporations. It is also clear that these organizations would be impotent without taxpayer funds and governmental cooperation, which helps explain why the authorities do not recognize the poverty of Washington's citizens as a dilemma: impoverished residents are not the constituency being served.

That the government is willing but unable to serve or govern its constituents seems almost more disconcerting than the corruption inherent to the previous argument. The most damning evidence here is that Washington D.C., following years of direct oversight by a government with abundant resources, resembles, in terms of wealth inequality and suffering, a third world capital. The power elite in D.C. are well aware of the impoverishment that surrounds them; they know the poor people are present because -in addition to walking by them everyday- the federal politicians are their appointed guardians. There is nowhere else to look for accountability. Even if they are 'willing' to serve, the federal authorities of the earth's wealthiest country are failing and should be held directly responsible for the deplorable conditions of its capital city.

So ultimately the truth consists of a combination of these conclusions: Washington's citizens are ruled by a government unwilling and unable to govern or serve, divorced from basic moral and democratic principles. Now that we have seen that the government of Washington D.C. is not "of, by or for the people," what is it?

To gauge the well-being of an organic creature one must check the health of its most vital organs. This analogy can be extended to nations as well. A capital city provides a tangible factor to examine the priorities, failures and successes of a society. Following the antecedent dissection of the capital, it is incontrovertible that Washington D.C. and the government which runs it are potent symbols which reflect the failing health of an entire society.

Poor and disenfranchised citizens throughout the U.S. suffer the same fate as their compatriots in D.C. They live in privation, with few middle class or ruling class comforts. Urban poor encounter astronomical levels of drugs, violence, hopelessness, crime and broken-down schools. The rural and suburban poor experience many comparable debilitating impediments. The cynicism and lack of governance displayed by the world's most powerful government towards Washington's less fortunate constituents mirrors the response of the authorities to the whole U.S. indigent population. Unwilling and unable to serve the poor, the government undemocratically lavishes gifts on the rich, the military and corporations.

Staunch democratic bankruptcy of the sort exhibited by the United States government appears nonsensical when compared to the official propagandized historical and mythical claims of democracy. Had the government of the United States ever honored the ideals of its democratically-inspired rhetoric, i.e. a "...government of the people, by the people, for the people..." Washington may have been a city lined with streets of gold, or, at the very least, a city of greatness. Instead it is the helm of an empire biding its time before it "...shall...perish from the earth."

WESTERN CIVILIZATION?

Now that we have traversed this short history of Western empires (and the capital of the current ruling empire), we can better distinguish the immorality which comprises the roots of their actions. We need to consider this legacy as it relates to myths of western "civilization." With all that has been discussed, it must be clear that the influence of said empires on the course of human history is not a myth. The strength of empires is in part reflected by their power to dictate their version of history, and, by extension, the history of those they have subjugated. It is through this biased recounting that western myths are disseminated. While it is true that Egypt, Rome and Great Britain all dramatically influenced history, the question becomes whether their actions created positive or negative outcomes. Contemplating what has already been asserted about these empires, one would have to assume that very little of what their rulers did would deserve praise or emulation. But that is exactly what we find in western mythology and in the contemporary legacy of the United States.

Today's mythmakers propagandize the legacy of these cultures through emphasis on the positive. Thus we are constantly reminded of these "civilizations'" glories and the debt that we owe them. Importance is placed on technological, artistic, scientific, governmental, and linguistic achievements. Note that the key word is emphasis. The point here is not to denigrate Egyptian artwork or Roman technology, but to take notice of the vast difference between the historians' focus on these cultural traits as opposed to imperial barbarism, cruelty, plunder and iniquity. All of which have negatively affected Western culture as much or more, than the commonly regaled positive characteristics.

More tragic than any of the foregoing mythmaking is the western empires' military legacy, adopted by the American Empire with a devotion equaling the depravity of these cultures' worst excesses. Without belaboring an argument that will be more fully explored in the following chapter, the parroting of militarism warrants mentioning. Atrocities committed by America's imperial forebears are presented in various ways, most of which downplay reality. For example, historians joyously recount the United States' cultural connection to the Romans, while they ignore or downplay Roman rapacity. Mainstream historians seldom acknowledge that there exists a tangible, continual link of brutality between all empires, and that the most potent legacy of these cultures is not great art and music, but inhumanity in its most exaggerated form.

Through this realization we arrive at the most insidious myth imparted on modern citizens of the earth: the myth of civilization. This myth, repeated in history texts, on television, in literature, in plays, in movies, in art galleries, and in governmental chambers, states that we Westerners are the blessed descendants of previous empires.[xii] But considering the immorality visited upon citizens, ancient and modern by these authorities, what then is the honest meaning of Western "civilization?" Beyond satisfying ruling class desires, what moral evolution has taken place in the wake of Western "civilization?" If the answer is troublesome to contemplate, we must then ask ourselves, who benefits from continuing the spectacle and the adoration?

To bring the point further, one must imagine what society might look like, if instead of constant invocations emphasizing the wonders of western empires, schoolchildren and adults received less biased teachings. Lessons including these empires' terrifying legacies would have a profound effect on the way people perceive the world. They may be more wary of perpetuating such a system, which could reciprocally help make the United States and the world a more peaceful and reflective place.

Tragically, the United States government is neither reflective nor peaceful. In living up to the precedent established by the empires reviewed here, the United States has continued to refine the imperial system and should furnish an iniquitous blueprint for future empires.

4

AMERICAN MILITARISM

*"Many parallels can be seen, moreover, between the
running of a regiment and that of a factory, each on hierarchical lines
and each with an often dehumanizing tendency to reduce
the human being to one machine among others."*

– V.G. KIERNAN

*"And it is for want of sufficiently distinguishing ideas,
and observing at how great a distance these people were from the first
state of nature, that so many authors have hastily concluded that man
is naturally cruel, and requires a civil government to make him more
gentle; whereas nothing is more gentle than he in his primitive state,
when placed by nature at an equal distance from the stupidity of brutes,
and the pernicious enlightenment of civilized man; and confined equally
by instinct and reason to providing against the harm which threatens
him, he is withheld by natural compassion from doing any injury to
others, so far from being led even to return that which he has received."*

– JEAN-JACQUES ROUSSEAU
Discourse on the Origin of Inequality

*"When all the world has become military,
then crime consists in not killing if orders insist on it."*

– ALBERT CAMUS
The Rebel

Because imperial militarism has been touched upon in the preceding analy-
ses, it may seem unnecessary to dedicate an entire chapter to the subject. [i]
However, my previous references provide only part of the information needed for
a methodical analysis of empires' militaristic behavior. Militarism occupies an
exalted place in the imperial mindset. It is through the military that empires gain
and exercise their power. Militarism has infected every empire in the history of

humanity, to the point where one must acknowledge its role as the characteristic that most often spurs imperial immorality.

With any subject of human concern there always exists a baseline from which to begin a discussion. In the case of militarism the baseline relates to the inevitability of human aggression. There are many who would argue that imperial militarism is inevitable because it simply reflects, on a grand scale, human beings' biological disposition towards violence. Accept this theory and one must accept the theory that not only are empires' massive militaries inevitable, but also a necessity. For if a state (empire or otherwise) has a military, others need one as well, if only for protection. However, using this argument to defend the existence of the military also reveals its flaws.

The primary fallacy of this argument surrounds the biological certainty of human aggression. There has never been, nor will there ever be a comprehensive study of humanity which determines that human beings are inherently violent. The reason this will never happen rests in its plain falsehood. If it were true, then the earth would be a much more violent place than it is today. Given the western media's obsessive fascination with violence, this may appear unfounded, but the truth is present in everyday reality. We must ask ourselves what percentage of the earth's inhabitants wake up every morning under the threat of violence. Without conducting a formal study, even the most jaundiced social scientist would have to admit the percentage is low. [ii]Conservatives who may be willing to admit that this is the case would note that the relative lack of violence emanates from the rule of law, i.e. nations' military and police establishments. I would argue that the relative lack of violence actually points to the native pacifism of humanity, and that rather than preventing violence, these military institutions, by their very nature, perpetuate violence.

The United States Empire has the most sophisticated, catastrophic military machine in the history of mankind and the authorities call it "defense." If the U.S. military is defensive and not a state-sponsored violence perpetuation mechanism, then the next logical questions become, defense for whom and against what?

In some ways, this simple language technicality helps unveil the myth of "inevitable" human aggression. "Defense" of such proportions is designed for intimidation at home and abroad. To answer the question as to who benefits from American militarism requires a bit more attention. And to uncover this is to uncover the core myth that sustains the empire's immorality. Unveiling this myth helps us recognize that unbridled, nationalistic human aggression does not occur "inevitably," but is a vital, systemic and sustaining feature of imperialism.

If an empire is to maintain and further its power, it must first (if the above assertions are correct) seek to establish for its military a place akin to godliness, where rejections or even doubts are seen as heretical. With the above parameters in place, analyzing the hallowed ground which supports the American military becomes easier and makes our societal subservience begin to appear sensible. And this is how we find the state of the military in today's American society. The military has been consecrated as a "sacred cow," rarely questioned, and at times even worshipped, by mainstream American culture.

BENEFICIARIES

Prior to delving into how such a drastic level of fidelity is achieved, it is important to determine who benefits most from the current American military configuration. The operative word here is "most." As we shall see, all classes of Americans have elements that view themselves as primary beneficiaries of our militarism. In this exploration it is important to separate out the actual beneficiaries from those who perceive themselves to be beneficiaries. Therefore by "most" I mean to pose a question which egalitarian-minded Americans, wary of allusions to class or overt control structures, have difficulty asking: whose power and money interests are most at stake in the perseverance and furtherance of the United States' military? The answer: any group or individual that derives a significant portion of their livelihood or power from America's global domination.

Let's put this definition to the test to see if we can more clearly delineate these beneficiaries. Does the governor of an Australian state qualify as a member of the club that benefits "most" from American militarism? This person benefits perhaps in the sense that Australia is a member state belonging to the West's domination of world capital (led by the U.S.). But, on the whole, they would not qualify. Does the governor of a random U.S. state, Maine, for example, qualify? In this instance the answer would have to be an unequivocal yes. Any Maine governor who did not overtly or covertly support institutions like the Bath Iron Works battleship construction facility, would not only undermine his or her own authority, but would also have no chance of being elected or re-elected. This same scenario would play out with regards to almost every congressional district or governorship. And so the answer for all of these politicians would also be a resounding yes.

What of the executives and major stockholders of corporations like General Electric, Boeing or GTE, which are three of the largest defense contractors in the United States? It should be clear that these individuals also have a very direct economic interest in preserving the American military apparatus. What of the U.S. executive branch of government, whose head (the President) serves as the armed forces Commander in Chief, and whose various members (head of the National Security Council, the Secretary of State, the Secretary of Defense, etc.) are intimately connected with the Pentagon's operation? Surely one would have to say that these people are fully vested in the military, and that they are among those who benefit "most" from its existence (as evidenced by their easy movement between their governmental roles and the boards of major defense contractors). How about the leaders of European governments, who wear the yoke of the American military around their necks in the form of NATO? They too, would have to be described as true (albeit at times, begrudging) beneficiaries. The most important list of potential benefactors is reserved for the high-ranking officers, bureaucrats and executives of America's myriad "security" agencies (FBI, CIA, NSA, etc.) and military branches (Army, Navy, Air Force, Marines, NASA, National Guards, the Coast Guard, etc.). These people unquestionably profit, both literally and figuratively, through the promotion of U.S. militarism.

Of course there are countless examples where an immediate answer to the question does not come readily. In cases such as the large shareholders and executives at McDonald's, where massive benefits are certainly realized from America's global hegemony, they would not, in some peoples eyes, necessarily warrant the title of benefiting "most" from U.S. military imperialism. In such situations, one needs to ask if these people would enjoy the same level of prosperity and authority were it not for American military power. And while McDonald's executives and top shareholders may not be in the same position as those at GE, it can be said that they derive vital benefits from the current U.S. regime. These less formal, yet essential, interconnections between America's military and corporate oligarchs (like McDonalds) will be discussed more fully in the next chapter.

One may wonder, in the foregoing questions, why the dividends were attributed exclusively to high-ranking officers, politicians and executives, and not to the more humble citizens who toil at Boeing's weapons factories or in some mindless mid-level Pentagon office job. To wholly understand the reasoning behind the emphasis I have placed here, one must take into consideration not just those who benefit from U.S. militarism, but also who and what these very same authorities would have us believe it benefits.

The paramount concern of pro-military propagandists and mythmakers is that the true beneficiaries of the system are either never revealed, or, if this proves impossible, that they be de-emphasized. Convincing the average citizen that they are the military system's true beneficiaries occupies the highest order in authoritarian methodology. Establishing such an illusion helps tremendously in the tasks mentioned above, for if a non-invested person can be convinced that he or she is, in fact, invested, other control mechanisms are almost unnecessary.[iii]

One way of looking at this reality is to examine the total number of American war casualties. From 1775 until the present, the estimated number of American war fatalities is over 1 million, with almost 42 million participants (U.S Department of Veterans Affairs). The death toll does not include colonists and Native Americans who perished fighting against each other before the Revolutionary War, or those who suffered grave mental and physical injuries as a result of combat. Those in command at the time of these numerous American wars generally claimed the fighting to be linked with the high ideals of freedom and democracy. But as we have seen from our previous discussions, America was never a democracy, nor was it ever free. Thus it is impossible for these to have been the impulses motivating the warfare. American empire building has led to the development of ever more abominable weapons and to American global military domination. Hardly linchpins of "freedom" or "democracy." Considering what we have observed regarding the general behavior and structure of empires, it would be contrary to its imperial nature for the United States to fight wars based on human ideals.

INDIVIDUAL ACCOUNTABILITY (REDUX)

Before investigating the other processes used by militarists to foment allegiance, one key point must be addressed. Some of those reading this analysis would surely balk at an explanation of militarism arising exclusively out of coercion and propaganda. He or she might argue that such a perspective smacks of "conspiracy" and gives the individual no responsibility for their personal conduct. With this in mind, and also because I believe this point of view has validity, we need to take a look at the individual's role in promoting militarism.

The narrative of U.S. militarism gains complexity the more closely one scrutinizes it. It would be simple enough if we had citizens and members of the military as passive agents, manipulated at will by the military's true beneficiaries. But this is not the entire picture. Since the claim here is that empires are unavoidably immoral and that the prime vehicle for this immorality is militarism, then surely some of our attention must focus upon those who follow orders. In the end, a vast network of individuals must support the immoral deeds of the military. The argument here is not that killing in and of itself is always an immoral proposition (although many pacifists believe it to be), but that killing for an empire whose operative impulses are necessarily and inevitably immoral, is. Therefore, killing, lending support to the killing machine, or using the threat of violence to promote the U.S. Empire, are all immoral. Which means any involved person or institution is morally culpable. This may appear to be a harsh appraisal, [iv]but when one considers the terrifying atrocities committed by the United States military, those who support the military, those who build the weapons and those who fire them must share the blame.

THE MESSAGE THROUGH MYTH

To this point we have touched briefly upon the unequal benefits doled out by the U.S. military. We have seen as well that the system has created believers from all classes of Americans, including its most disenfranchised citizens. We also established that due to the Empire's dissoluteness, there exists a tangible moral responsibility for those individuals involved in our imperial militancy. Key questions remain regarding the advancement of our national "sacred cow," for if the ruling class has indeed successfully convinced people who are not the true beneficiaries of militarism that they are, then there must surely be mechanisms -over and above enticements like mid-level jobs in the Pentagon or spots in the infantry- which keep everyone synchronized.

Let's focus on a few indispensable ways that myth and propaganda are used to promote American militarism. This focus should not be viewed as exclusionary; the examples which follow provide a only brief glimpse into what is an almost inexhaustible pool. To establish whether or not a pro-military mechanism falls in the category of myth or propaganda is somewhat difficult because the messages handed down by the authorities often function on both levels. For the purpose of this discussion I have chosen examples that I feel are more biased towards one function or the other.

For any cultural mythology, there must always be an underlying and accepted history from which it is derived. In the case of the United States, this legacy is specifically linked with handed-down beliefs surrounding American violence and militarism. America's mythmakers and propagandists would have citizens believe that all of our conflicts were fought for higher ideals, and never for profit, or power, or imperial expansion. However, to understand the Empire's current military condition and the factors that contribute to its survival, we need to deconstruct these sustaining myths.

Whether or not a person believes America was inevitably predestined to become an empire, it remains that from its inception on North American shores, individuals weaned on European imperialism were the same individuals who founded the United States. But our myths lead us away from this reality. In one commonly offered scenario, America's imperial desires did not begin in the 1600's, but in the late 1800's with the Spanish-American war. If one were to accept such an outlook, then America's entire history prior to this point would have to be ignored, or at least seriously modified.

For a strict military historian, any allegation that the United States was in any way a militarized state prior to the 20th century would be viewed with deep skepticism. The arguments set forth here will not focus on the size of American military apparatus, which inarguably grew to unimaginable levels of power during the 20th century (and coincided with the period of the Empire's most rapid expansion). Instead it will center on the continuous, historical efforts of European Americans to subjugate masses of people, whether native, imported Africans or foreigners.

A logical question behind such an examination is if the United States did not become a militarized state until the 20th century, then are not the historical mythmakers correct in placing America's imperial urge squarely in that century? No. Examples of U.S. military conquests prior to the Spanish-American War are numerous and fairly regular, pausing only briefly during the Civil War. [v] As discussed, the violence of white Europeans against the east coast Native Americans began almost as soon as the colonists arrived in North America. This aggression continued throughout the period of America's continental expansion. If U.S. wars directed at Native Americans failed to extirpate them from a part of the country, then they were put under governmental removal programs (Wolfe 1982, p. 285). This imperialist behavior can be seen with black Americans as well. While governmentally condoned slavery ended in 1865, state-sponsored discrimination persisted until the 1960s, and systemic white racism towards (and attempted domination over) black Americans continues to this day. There are also multiple examples of pre-Spanish American War imperial interactions with other nations.[vi]

America's urge to empire, expressed through its military pursuits, did not appear spontaneously, incongruous with its formally disinterested stance. The United States was busy building its empire long before the Spanish-American war, which was simply one more congruous attempt to add additional people, places and resources to its expanding line of control.

The mythology surrounding American militarism presents itself in other cultural forms besides the perpetuation of false history. When considering America's military establishment, perhaps the most important rituals are holiday and memorial traditions. Military holidays and memorials are, by and large, mythological in nature. They are not mythological in that they celebrate soldiers who did not fight, or wars that did not happen, they are mythological because they celebrate and glorify the Empire's aggression. Their mythological quality stems from an inherent contradiction. For while they claim to patriotically honor those who willingly and unwillingly served, their actual (unstated) purpose is to ensure the Empire's supremacy, which can only be achieved through coercion of the populace.

For instance, would all of those individuals who died in American acts of aggression support the multitudinous memorials and holidays held in their honor? Would all those who were victimized by American wars support these occasions? If any of the living or the dead were to answer no to these questions, then they end up doubly persecuted, first through their suffering or death, and second through the celebration of war in their unsanctioned honor. While no comprehensive poll has been taken of our deceased or living veterans (or their victims), my guess is that tens, perhaps hundreds of thousands, experienced a profound ambivalence towards state-sponsored violence, and that countless others had severe reservations, or antipathy towards their military assignments. It is possible that many veterans would actually prefer peace memorials, because they know, better than non-veterans, the true cost of war.

The next logical question is whether or not those who currently (and historically) benefit "most" from American militarism, i.e. the commander-in-chief, the CEO of Raytheon, state governors, Pentagon warlords, etc., have any ambivalent feelings around military holidays and memorials? If these individuals felt uncertainty about such events, it would have to fall into the category of biting the hand that feeds. In other words, if you were a manufacturer of kites and there were numerous governmentally endorsed kite holidays, in addition to thousands of kite statues and memorials throughout the country, what conflicted interest could you possibly have if your goal was to sell more kites? The same must be asked of our manufacturers of war. What possible contradictory emotions could they possibly have regarding celebrations which so intimately benefit their monetary and power concerns? Ultimately, those who start wars and those who profit the from U.S. militarism (and who generally do not suffer or pay with their lives) are the authentic beneficiaries of these observances. They have little to lose, and everything to gain from their perpetuity.

THE MESSAGE THROUGH PROPAGANDA

Turning our attention to pro-military propaganda methods, one sees them most acutely displayed by the mainstream press during U.S. military conflicts. I in no way wish to minimize the larger sycophancy of the media. The fact that they are wedded to imperialism (and to the beneficent American Empire) provides an automatic bias in any "news" reporting they do. In considering the first Iraq War, I have chosen a five-day stretch of *New York Times* coverage to illuminate the cunning nature of mainstream American war reporting. *The New York Times* was selected based on its unique status as both a revered and reviled entity. The paper maintains a dedicated following of liberal-minded Americans who feel that its coverage is erudite, balanced and well-informed. The paper is reviled by many conservatives, and is often cited by them as an example of leftwing bias in the media. By dispensing these commonly held assessments, we should be able to discern the *Times* honest purpose.

The five-days of coverage begins on January 17th, 1991, the first day of the Gulf War, through the following Monday. There exists no reason for selecting these days, other than there being ample war stories to analyze. My contention remains that any period of media reporting on the Gulf War (or any war) from a mainstream publication would substantiate the following claims.

Before entering into this brief analysis, certain assumptions must be noted to help contextualize my argument. The first major assumption is that the purpose of the news media is not only to report verbatim facts, but also to critically assess those facts to the best of their ability. A corresponding assumption is that to be considered factual, news information must not exclusively rely upon official sources, which is a technique that helps reporters avoid bias. The final assumption is that human events do not occur in historical vacuums. This means, for example, that confrontations between nation-states always evolve from a set of historical variables, and these variables must be discussed to make sense of preconditions that lead to conflict. If these assumptions are not met, or are not taken seriously, then the news of a media outlet must be considered illegitimate propaganda, especially if said information reaches large numbers of a given populace as truth.

None of these assumptions are met in this five-day sample period of *New York Times'* Gulf War coverage. On the initial day of the bombing, numerous articles were written. The front page pieces of the *Times* fixate on the conclusion of our long wait to expel Iraqi forces from Kuwait, and on official portrayals of the United States' military offensive (*The New York Times* 1/17/91, p. 1). Beyond pat descriptions of American military involvement and executive branch regurgitation (i.e. "Defense" Secretary Cheney's statement that targets were selected to "avoid injury to civilians" - *The New York Times* 1/17/91, p. 1), little substantive historical or critical analysis is presented. For instance, the fact that up until the late 1980's Saddam Hussein was a pawn for U.S. Mid-East policy, or that Iraq received millions in U.S. military and financial aid (all while George Bush Sr. was a top member of America's executive branch), merits no mention. Additionally, the Middle East's importance as a reservoir for U.S. oil consumption, and America's coinciding necessity to militarily control the region is never broached. Finally, no unofficial or neutral sources, or criticisms are cited.

Later in the same newspaper, diagrams of Iraqi and American military machinery appear on page 15, along with a myopic, seemingly officially-sanctioned insider's report on Bush's "matter-of-fact" and "calm" decision to wage war on page 16 (*The New York Times* 1/17/91, p. 15 & 16). Under the above-established assumptions of what comprises actual news reporting versus propaganda, *The New York Times* first day of Gulf War coverage falls squarely into the category of propaganda.

The second day of "reporting" echoes that of the first, with the notable twist of Iraq sending Scud missiles into Israel. This is not to say that such a development was unexpected by the American or Israeli authorities, but just that *The New York Times'* "reports" shift in this direction (*The New York Times* 1/18/91, p. 1). Once again, the historical reasons underlying U.S. support (and thus mainstream media concern) for the well-being of Israel are presented as a preordained fact which, "...Complicates U.S. Strategy in Gulf" to quote part of one article's headline (*The New York Times* 1/18/91, p. 1). The void of even a quick note regarding America's quite potent and relevant history with Israel, and Israel's utterly dependent relationship with the U.S. government (similar to Iraq's relationship with the U.S. prior to the Gulf War), would make it difficult for an uninformed person to understand the newspaper's alarm. But, as with the first day's stories, the newspaper's expressed fears and the fears of the U.S. authorities are largely interchangeable, due to *The New York Times'* almost exclusive reliance on "official" sources. Again, the "news" delivered by *The New York Times* lacks characteristics which would distinguish it from propaganda.

For those who might balk at the assumptions I have used to separate news from propaganda, the third day of *New York Times'* coverage offers evidence that its editors understand the difference. In Saturday's Gulf War reporting (1/19/91), the paper's overseers tacitly admit to recognizing the importance of impartial information. A small, inconspicuous, self-contained box on page 6, with the heading, "Censors Screen Pooled Reports" reads:

> *The American-led military command in Saudi Arabia has put into effect press restrictions under which journalists are assembled in small groups and given access to various military sources. These pool reporters obtain their information while under military escort, and their accounts are subject to scrutiny by military censors before they are distributed. Much of the information in articles today on American military operations was obtained under such circumstances. (The New York Times 1/19/91, p. 6)*

The inconceivable aspect about such a revelation is that up to this point and continuing on this day's coverage, the use of American officials for the bulk of their source material had gone unnoted. And even though this little blurb is tucked away on page 6, it provides a glimpse into the editors' consciences and proves that they were, at the very least, vaguely aware of their responsibility to function as a news organization, not a propaganda organ.[vii]

Given their near confession of guilt and acknowledgement of proper journalistic protocol, coverage on day three can be seen as even more reactionary. The front-page articles provide more of the same: unquestioned, official versions of the war, fears for Israeli safety and fears that they will enter the war, and thus foil the U.S. agenda (*The New York Times* 1/19/91, p. 1). An article entitled "Computerized Accuracy: 'A Relief to See the Tomahawks Fly'" adjacent to the censorship blurb on page 6, offers a basic dose of military glorification, with statements (like the one quoted in the title) from American military personnel representing the story's main content. More alarming still is an article on page 37 of the business section, titled, "Pride of a Texas Plant: The Fast and Agile F-16," which reads:

> *And, like workers at military equipment plants across the country, the 24,000 employees building F-16's at the General Dynamics plant here find themselves rooting for their products and the Americans operating them with a blend of pride, confidence and worry that they never felt before. (The New York Times 1/19/91, p. 37)*

With statements like this, loaded with such concerted and obvious propaganda functions, it would be hard to fathom the American authorities ever needing to fret about the dangers of too much press freedom.

Undifferentiated from the previous two days of "news," the third day of reporting on the Gulf War fails in all three categories that distinguish news from propaganda. There exists little critical analysis, a marked absence of unofficial sources and a paucity of historical information.

In the interest of looking at a wider sample of data, let's consider the fourth and fifth days of *New York Times'* "news." Sunday's war reporting marks a continued adherence to the *Times'* propaganda methods. The front-page articles are concerned with reiterating Pentagon renderings of the war (with the *Times* still willingly publishing censored material), which are increasingly focused on the potential dangers of a future ground war. A story entitled, "U.S. War Plan: Still the Ground to Conquer," warns the reader of the Iraqi's "formidable Republican Guard troops and top Iraqi tank divisions" (*The New York Times* 1/20/91, p. 1). As evidenced by the eventual wholesale American slaughter of the Iraqi ground forces, one must surmise that there were other reasons for the military to promote, and for *The New York Times* to print, such erroneous information. Other front-page pieces focus on the possibility of Israeli involvement and on the F.B.I. remaining vigilant against internal terrorist threats (*The New York Times* 1/20/91, p. 1).

Buried deep in their Sunday coverage is an article entitled, "Press and U.S. Officials at Odds on News Curbs" (*The New York Times* 1/20/91, p. 16), describing a supposed difference of opinion between the press and the government over the control of information. Again, that the editors of the *Times* find it necessary to print a story on this subject should be seen as instructive, given that up to this point, the vast majority of their "news" had come via virtually unquestioned official sources. The author even goes so far as to quote the *Times'* executive editor, who says, "We are not getting any information that really fully and properly describes the [war's] magnitude..." (*The New York Times* 1/20/91, p. 16).

Contained within this same piece are hypocritical assertions such as, "Journalists now mistrust the Government and especially the military in large part because of their experience of having been deceived in Vietnam." (*The New York Times* 1/20/91, p. 16) Where in *The New York Times'* coverage has this skepticism, so crucial to unbiased reporting, been in evidence? And would not the almost total censorship of the press indicate an even greater deception than that practiced by the military during Vietnam? The article also contains a bit of misguided mud-slinging at television stations reporting on the war. The author states, "At the same time, journalists, particularly on television, have periodically failed to distinguish fact from rumor, and the public has received false and misleading reports." (*The New York Times* 1/20/91, p. 16) This observation is not misguided because it is untruthful; rather, it is one more inadvertent admission of *The New York Times'* failure as a news organization. For this statement to be true, only the singling out of television reporting needs redacting.

The final day of "news" coverage in this analysis warrants attention mainly because *The New York Times'* propaganda campaign persists undiminished, with only officially sanctioned, one-sided, non-historical, non-analytical stories covering the front page (*The New York Times* 1/21/91, p. 1). The twist on day five was the Iraqi capture of prisoners, which is described as making one Pentagon officer "numb" after she listened to an audio tape of their interrogation (*The New York Times* 1/21/91, p. 1).

Thomas Friedman's piece entitled, "Hard Times, Better Allies" appears, at first glance, to be historical in nature, thus threatening to violate the premise that such information was absent from the *Times'* coverage of the war. The brunt of his story is that since the start of the war (and the ensuing missile attacks on Israel by Iraq), the relationship between the United States and Israel had "strikingly improved" according to American and Israeli "officials" (*The New York Times* 1/21/91, p. 1). He goes on to say that:

> ...*these officials are keenly aware that the recent sensitivity the two countries are showing and American soldiers' participation, for the first time, in the defense of Israel, derive primarily from a coincidence of strategic interests and not from an outburst of mutual concern. If those interests change, so might some of those good feelings.* (*The New York Times* 1/21/91, p. 1)

His faux-historical reporting is actually more dangerous than if the *Times* had simply left history off its agenda. It is dangerous because Mr. Friedman is rewriting history to fit a story line. Regardless of what the day-to-day relationship of the two countries' leaders is, the fact remains that Israel had been, and was at this point, a client state of America, to whom we gave billions in arms, money and nuclear technology, so that they would in turn be beholden to the United States' Middle East interests. Friedman fairly admits as much when he cites incidents of the Israelis taking military action, "...without considering American interests or always giving Washington prior notification" (*The New York Times* 1/21/91, p. 1) as evidence of the strained pre-Gulf War U.S.-Israeli relationship. That it is understood and accepted by Friedman and *The New York Times* that Israel must play the role of obedient child provides sufficient evidence alone to debunk his phony history.

On page 10 of Monday's paper, there is another story about the relationship between the U.S. press and the military (*The New York Times* 1/21/91, p. 10). This report is noteworthy on several different levels. The first is that the reporter has contradictory feelings around military censorship. He describes some correspondents as, "...bridling under a system of conflicting rules and confusing censorship." (*The New York Times* 1/21/91, p. 10) Later in the article he states, "Most reporters are uncomfortable with a news system so completely under military control." (*The New York Times* 1/21/91, p. 10) But, in a more conciliatory mood, he says that "Most [reporters] accept such constraints without protest" and that "Most journalists here agree that military information officers at the Joint Information Bureau in Dhahran are helpful and fair." (*The New York Times* 1/21/91, p. 10)

Perhaps the more fascinating attribute of this article is that it describes how the process of censorship takes place. Reporters are given subjects hand-picked by the military; then their stories are reviewed by the military censors in Saudi Arabia, and then by censors in Washington. In an example provided by the author, a *Times'* reporter, "To hasten the transmission of the news," agrees to military changes in an article, "...so that American publications and news services could receive it in time for deadlines." (*The New York Times* 1/21/91, p. 10) Ultimately, this reporter's servility did not help, as the article, approved by the local command, was rejected by Washington and was only allowed to go to print a day later, when the news, "...had become stale." (*The New York Times* 1/21/91, p. 10)

What paramount contributing factor led to the befuddled nature of this short piece? It is the author's capitulation to his military handlers that exposes the gap between claims of journalistic integrity and the actual state of being a propaganda flack for U.S. imperialism.

The terms of this very limited critique of military censorship bears no resemblance to news agencies' supposed "mistrust" of the military discussed in the *Times'* previous days' paper. Especially considering that, "...correspondents must submit to near total military supervision of their work." (*The New York Times* 1/21/91, p. 10) The debate over information and censorship is confined to information on air strikes or missile launchings, and never with any fundamental questioning of U.S. behavior or involvement.

If these repeated attempts to justify its behavior were not buried so deeply within the coverage, or if the stories got to the heart of the matter and admitted directly *The New York Times'* role as a propaganda vehicle, then perhaps it would be easier to overlook its failings as a news agency. We must remember that *The New York Times* was chosen as an example of mainstream press compliance due to its twofold status as a bastion of liberalism (according to many American conservatives) and as a bastion of intellectualism (according to many American liberals). Considering the obsequiousness that pervades *The New York Times'* war coverage it is alarming that large swaths of the population believe in the paper's journalistic reliability. More importantly, it is a testament to how well the *Times* fulfills its prescribed purpose as a vehicle for furthering the propaganda of the imperial regime.

If the foregoing conclusions regarding the intimate relationship between the propaganda of the press and the military are seen as insufficient, then I would encourage anyone to use the same formula and apply it to a random five-day period of mainstream media Gulf War (or Afghanistan, Iraq II, etc.) reporting. If my underlying assumptions relating to unbiased news reporting are deemed unfair, then apply even less stringent analytical guidelines. The results, I am confident, will be the same.

BIGGER THAN BIG

While it is true that all empires possess, as a rule, an insatiable desire for domination, the present-day U.S. military deserves a quick look, if only for the freakish nature of its proportions.

The defense budget at the time of this writing is more than 400 billion dollars a year, with hundreds of thousands of troops stationed abroad.[viii] Not including the already referenced post-World War II multi-trillion dollar nuclear budget, the United States spent an additional 13.2 trillion dollars on other military concerns from 1940-1996 (Schwartz, 1998). Although such an inconceivable level of resource dedication should alone be adequate for revealing the current Empire's rapacity, there exists another frightening manifestation of the American military phenomena. The military, following the Empire's rapid 20th century expansion, has now reached a point of animism. To affirm this we must observe how the military justifies itself in its own words.

In looking at the Pentagon's self-perception, I have chosen its year 2000

Annual Report To the President and the Congress. The document has many fascinating characteristics, the most interesting of which are its persistent self-justifications. Warnings to the President and Congress about impending threats to American security pervade the document's text. On the first page of chapter one, entitled, "The Defense Strategy," there are references to America facing "...a dynamic and uncertain security environment" and that "...the world remains a complex, dynamic, and dangerous place (www.dtic.mil/execsec/adr2000/chap1.html, p. 1)." Note how the writer(s) assumes the reader accepts these claims at face value, even as the United States military is the largest in the world, bar none, that hundreds of billions of dollars spent on militarism represents a "defense" of any kind and that countries on the brink of starvation, such as North Korea, represent the aforementioned security "uncertainties." If untruths of this magnitude can be offered by the Pentagon with a straight face, work towards achieving compliance with its wants is all but guaranteed.

Just three pages into the report, the Pentagon's true motives are laid bare. Under a heading labeled, "The Imperative of Engagement," the report clearly states that "...over the next 15 to 20 years [the U.S.], ...will maintain its capability as a world-class military power" and that were the U.S. "...to withdraw from its international commitments, ...or forfeit its military preeminence, the world would become an even more dangerous place." (www.dtic.mil/execsec/adr2000/chap1.html, p. 3) The most important and significant revelation here is the military's rationalization of its own animate existence. The idea that without an outlandishly funded American military, the world would be "even more dangerous" should be a preposterous notion. But this is an interesting use of psychology: first we need the military due to the danger of the world, and secondly, the military secures the world against further danger. Never is a hint provided in these assertions as to the historical role the American military has played in destabilizing the world and America itself, nor to the blatantly illogical nature behind the self-justification. The only surprising aspect of these declarations is the 15 to 20 year time frame, presumably an attempt at imperial modesty.

Two other notable features in the report relate to foreign affairs and the spread of the American elite's version of globalization, both of which bear ramifications for the following chapters. The first concerns the manner by which the military wishes to guarantee "democracy," and the concept that militarism in some way equates or guarantees freedom abroad. Examples of this logic can be found in the first chapter of the report: "Military contacts with non-democratic or newly democratic countries promote democratization... ," or "The Department of Defense promotes regional stability by facilitating regional cooperation, supporting democratization, and enhancing transparency with potential adversaries." (www.dtic.mil/execsec/adr2000/chap1.html, p. 5) One would have to assume, with so many examples pointing to the exact opposite historical role of the U.S. military, that perhaps the authors view America's position as the world's largest exporter of arms, or our training and support of brutal reactionary regimes (for over 60 years the U.S. run School of the Americas has trained thousands of Latin American soldiers in the art of killing, destabilizing democracy and assassination) as evidence of the military's faith in democracy. Within the context of the military's stated tactics of promoting "democracy," i.e., its forces "...permanently stationed abroad..." (www.dtic.mil/execsec/adr2000/chap1.html, p. 5) and "...the unilateral use of military power..." (ibid, p. 4), it would also be difficult to understand how other countries would feel comfortable with this brand of freedom.

The second feature is the clearly stated role of the U.S. military as the bully behind the spread of American pseudo-capitalism. If one were to have doubts that the current world economic system finds its sustenance in the threat of violence via the American military, a quick look at the report should dispel any questions. The report contains multiple references to the military's role in propping up U.S. capitalism. One such quote is that the military must ensure that "The global economy and free trade are growing" (ibid, p. 1). Another is that

"The United States will remain engaged abroad, supporting efforts to enlarge the community of secure, free-market, and democratic nations and to create new partners in peace and prosperity." (ibid, p. 3) Undoubtedly the current global economic system would look very different if not for the Empire's favorite instrument of repression.

Throughout this report there are countless other examples of the Pentagon's "logic." If such Orwellian language can be employed by the military with impunity, then why, beyond the section where the yearly billions are discussed, are the reports even necessary? That the Pentagon still feels a need to justify (albeit incoherently) its behavior is perhaps the one hopeful sign in the whole exercise.

The only way to make these observations on the U.S. military comprehensible is to view them contextually, within the imperial system. Such a shocking amount of money, time and energy spent in the name of killing can be realized only through the powerful application of myth and propaganda by militarism's true beneficiaries, and through the complicity of millions of average Americans (false beneficiaries), who directly and indirectly support the terrible injustice of it all.

During the writing of this chapter, the attacks on the World Trade Center and the Pentagon occurred. There will be ample dissection of these events, but they are worth considering within context of this discussion. Most notably: the lack of critical analysis or any measurable dissent by the major news outlets (more drastic than the Gulf War coverage); the use of patriotism and nationalism to justify American atrocities at home and abroad; a profound inability of the imperial elite to either admit their partial complicity in the attacks, or the actual reasons for the Empire's unilateral retaliation.[ix x] All of these facets are consistent with the findings in this chapter.

VIOLENCE AND GREED: GLOBALIZATION AND NEO-COLONIALISM

*"...at the same time, the supernumerary inhabitants, who were
too weak or too indolent to make such acquisitions in their turn,
impoverished without having lost anything, because while everything
about them changed they alone remained the same, were obliged
to receive or force their subsistence from the hands of the rich.
And from that began to arise, according to their different characters,
domination and slavery, or violence and rapine. The rich on their side
scarcely began to taste the pleasure of commanding, when they preferred it
to every other; and making use of their old slaves to acquire new ones,
they no longer thought of anything but subduing and enslaving their
neighbors; like those ravenous wolves, who having once tasted human
flesh, despise every other food, and thereafter want only men to devour."*

– JEAN-JACQUES ROUSSEAU
Discourse on the Origin of Inequality

*"Invitations to seek private satisfaction or consolation or wealth or power
come relentlessly to us in these times, at the expense almost always
of the public and the communal, whose invitations are weak
and uncertain and filled with doubt, and lacking
in the high-budget promotional certainties of the age."*

– STANLEY CRAWFORD
A Garlic Testament

It may seem odd to dedicate an entire chapter to private enterprise given that up to this point we have focused primarily on governmental deficiencies, but the picture would not be complete without due attention to the corporations that occupy the very epicenter of American imperialism. Just as our massive military machine is geared towards murder, large corporations are geared towards greed, backed by violence, at whatever cost to humanity or the environment. This section will address these costs, and will attempt to unveil the historical and contemporary factors which contribute to the system's continuance. It will also dissect the myths surrounding the concepts of "competitive" and "cooperative" as they relate to economics, and try to point out the negligible difference between the "public" and "private" sectors of the American economy.

THE RAMIFICATIONS OF EUROPEAN COLONIALISM

Empires from the Egyptian to the Roman all had, as a core axiom, the consolidation of power and resources for the ruling elite's advantage. Prior to the sophisticated colonization tactics of the European powers, many ancient civilizations dominated other peoples and cultures by trade or military coercion.

While ancient empires did everything within their power to control as many resources as possible, this goal was not realized on a global scale until the era of European colonization beginning in the 16th century. With advances in ocean transport and navigation, Europeans discovered new parts of the globe. The discovery of new lands brought contact with a myriad of cultures, many of which were quite advanced. What the European elite saw in these peoples was a tremendous opportunity for exploitation. While many of the societies were sophisticated, few had the ability to withstand the twin assault of European guns and diseases. By the 18th century the European powers (especially Great Britain) had jumped from global discovery to global suzerainty.[i]

The reference to the 18th century is important because it marks the beginning of the industrial revolution. With the advent of mechanization and the development of factory systems, particularly in England, the need for raw materials from the British Empire's conquered territories became more urgent than ever before. Resources and space were limited on the British Isles (and in other European nations) so the ruling classes needed outside resources to quench their desire for profits. And in this they succeeded, as the colonial industrial era led to the largest concentrations of capital in the history of humankind. For the men who led these European companies and empires, subduing, enslaving, raping and pillaging the native populations were, to some degree, incidental to their desire for economic preeminence. [ii] Colonialism was considered an efficacious method of realizing a profit, and the goods and labor supplied by the subjugated were what made this possible. It must also be noted that vassalage on such a large scale would not have been possible without the assistance of the various empires' militaries, a condition which persists to this day.

Eventually, as with people's resistance to ruling class policies in America, the human beings in these countries did become a factor in hastening the end of colonialism, much to the consternation of European rulers. Although their insubordination was not the main determinant in dismantling European colonialism (World War II was perhaps a greater factor), it did in many cases quicken the subjugators' exit, and gradually, in the decades following World War II, one colonial possession after another slipped from European control.

The tragic impact of colonialism did not end with its geographical disintegration. Although not all former colonies are failing nations, the majority are. It would be shortsighted to blame these failings entirely upon the Europeans (examples of ruthless dictators and corrupt regimes are abundant enough in the post-colonial world), but certainly substantial fault does lie with the colonial governments. Still, the most pertinent aspect of colonialism is not necessarily historical; it is the legacy of colonialism embodied in neo-colonialism that most strongly affects present-day economics. In other words, the Europeans and Americans have replaced the old system of exploitation through physical occupation, with exploitation via globalization. Some of the tools for this latest form of domination are new, exemplified by organizations like the World Bank, the WTO and the IMF; some, like the military, remain all too familiar. However, the net results for poor countries have not changed and ramifications such as the destruction of native cultures, environmental degradation and economic coercion, are all consistent with colonialism. The bottom line is that globalization (regardless of what today's first-world rulers tell us) does not represent a bold new way: it's merely imperial control via new means. Globalization is the modern expression of an antiquated and reactionary economic system, skeletally unchanged for the past 500 years.

Given the tumultuous social changes which have occurred over the past 500 years, the relative stagnancy of world economics is astounding.[iii]One key reason why the system has changed so little rests in the fact that those who have reaped the spoils have been unwilling to loosen the reins. Therefore, we have the present system of globalization (i.e. a neo-colonial ruling-elite economy) vociferously backed by the richest countries on earth, when, not unexpectedly, the average income in the wealthiest 20 nations is 37 times that of the world's 20 poorest (World Bank 2003) and according to World Institute for Development Economics Research, in the year 2000 the richest 1% of the world's adult population owned 40% of its wealth and the bottom half owned around 1% of the earth's assets.

What does it mean to say that the world's dominant economic structure has barely changed in the past 500 years? By investigating the contemporary economy's global manifestations one can witness what little betterment for the earth's majority has taken place since the time of early European colonialism. We will see that rather than having a decentralizing or democratizing effect on human existence, globalization impedes both.

GLOBALIZATION AND VIOLENCE

Today, the pseudo-capitalist economic system rules the planet. There do exist alternate examples throughout the world of smaller economic models that differ from the prevailing paradigm (i.e. Communism, cooperatives, socialistic, dictatorships, etc.) but the focus here will be on the predominant model.

As we further dissect this relationship between the American global military posture and globalization, an important question must be kept in mind. Now that the presence of the Soviet Union can no longer be used to justify imperial military excesses, what can? If all of these horrible weapons of hate and destruction were rationalized as a defense against communism, what is the rationalization now? And if there are suspicions that the perennial billions spent on the U.S. military may not all be for "defense" against "terrorists" or "rogue states," then perhaps the Empire has some less commonly propagandized reasons for the military's supremacy.

Of course, one reason for such excess is to impress upon the world, via threats, influence and direct force, the dominance of large-scale pseudo-capitalism. [iv]The following are just a few examples of techniques that are deployed to insure globalization's hegemony.

The most obvious example of the American threat can be seen in its military presence encircling the globe. The implication of this posture is that the American Empire can rapidly respond to any challenges to globalization with violence, anywhere on earth, at a moment's notice. The incessant war on Iraq is an example of America using direct force to aid its economic ideology. By constantly attacking Iraq, a country with the second largest petroleum reserves on the planet -but one which had also violated its warm relations with the United States- the Empire is able to gain some control over world oil supplies, which in turn assists American (and British) oil companies. Additionally, the empire arms and supports reactionary U.S.-friendly regimes the world over. (Johnson, p. 53-58, 2003) This works well for pro-globalization governments. Because, as in the cases of Israel, Egypt, Kuwait and Saudi Arabia, the Empire gains sympathetic, armed allies, in a region of great energy resources and limited American-friendly populations. These governments provide the added bonus of suppressing anti-American and anti-globalization sentiments within their own borders.

It must also briefly be mentioned that the "defense" industry itself is a growing, massive corporate entity, with over 3000 federal contracts worth more than 300 billion dollars over the past decade alone (The Center for Public Integrity, 2002). In addition to the innumerable public dollars which fund research, subsidies and tax breaks for this industry, countries such as Israel, Saudi Arabia, Qatar (and numerous others) offer the United States' government a two-for-one special. They act both as repressive American client states and support the Empire's dearest companions, the defense and petroleum industries.[v]

There is a vital link between the "free-market" economy, multinational corporations, and the United States military. It is important to understand that the class of people who run this economy, both in the U.S. and abroad, are not politically distinguishable. While the Democrats and Republicans perform their dance, they never disagree on sacraments like the imperial economy or the military, and more often than not attempt to outdo each other in demonstrating their allegiance to these constructs.[vi]

The majority of those in the political class, along with defense and oil company executives, would have to be viewed as benefiting directly from globalization, either through money or power interests. (The enormous taxpayer-funded and subsidized, non-competitive contracts issued for the current rebuilding of Iraq, are but one glaring example.) As discussed, there are myriad other beneficiaries of the American military posture, including the managerial class in most multinational and global media companies. And while they are not the obvious players of the defense and oil managers, they are vitally connected nonetheless. As long as executives at McDonald's and *The New York Times* feel they are getting a piece of the action, there exists little cause for dissent from the system. Like the Roman imperial class before them, the present-day elite dominates the political landscape, the only difference being that their power has become global in scale.

Before moving on to the myth behind the present "competitive," "capitalist" economies, two other issues regarding the ruling-elite economy must be addressed. The first is a rebuttal to what is often asserted whenever a ruling class gets mentioned. Some would claim that any theory having to do with the existence of a group of covert rulers is, by its very nature, a conspiracy theory, and thus a fallacy. My response to this line of reasoning is that I do not happen to believe that the elite, by gathering in private clubs (The World Economic Forum, The Bilderberg Group, etc.) to discuss how they will divide the spoils, drives the machine. Instead,

I believe there are sufficient shared power and monetary interests that secret societies are somewhat unnecessary for the elite to be on similar footing.

The second issue has to do with class. In America "class" is a dirty word. Many in the middle and upper classes have come to see the present era as a time devoid of class structure. This flies in the face of reality as evidenced by the United Sates' hierarchically ordered, iniquitous, rampantly materialistic society. But, this fantasy of a classless society, regardless of how it has become ingrained in the United States' mass consciousness also helps to maintain the economic status quo.

PASSIVE COOPERATION

The irony of course is that the U.S.-led globalization system could not accurately be called either capitalist or competitive. Since both of these attributes are viewed by the general public as fundamental to our economic system, the prevailing absence of either deserves some attention.

Passive cooperation, not competition, represents the dominant force in today's world economy. Because the majority of citizens in the developed world do not live on cooperative farms or industrial communes, we have come to believe (once again, not without further help from various mythmakers) that life has much more to do with individualism than cooperation. But this is exactly why this myth is so insidious. First, it plays into the hands of those with control, by convincing the individual that he or she is a self-contained entity, dependent on very few external factors. And secondly, by extension, the myth persuades people that the nation-state (or empire) shares the same traits. Where would the United States government be without the willing assistance and cooperation of the taxpayer? Taxation may not exemplify an active form of cooperation, but it is an effective form of cooperation, and without it, any state would be powerless.

If one were to accept the notion that at its center the United States is one large, passive cooperative, then surely multinational corporations would represent the antithesis, and should be considered, as we have been led to believe, paragons of competition. This too is a deeply embedded and ultimately false myth. Without the U.S. military in the Middle East, oil companies would not be able to secure foreign oil. Without willing, publicly supported regimes the world over, the defense industry would hardly exist. Without trees from publicly owned lands, timber companies would fold in a matter of weeks, and so on. And, if one subtracts publicly-funded aid, subsidies, research monies, government contracts, bailouts, bonds, tax breaks, tariffs, and all the other legislated handouts, what conglomerate would retain anywhere near its current level of dominion?

Although these multinationals could not exist without public welfare and cooperation, we in the developed world can at least assure ourselves that we do live in capitalist (albeit non-competitive) societies. It is imperative that we believe this, in part because the moniker of capitalism gets employed to encourage the rest of the earth to do our bidding. But, analogous to other American fables, capitalism is also a false covenant.

Perhaps the best way uncover the capitalist myth is to take note of its definition in Merriam Webster's Collegiate Dictionary.

> **Capitalism** An economic system characterized by private or corporate ownership of capital goods, by investments that are determined by private decision, and by prices, production, and the distribution of goods that are determined mainly by competition in a free market

This definition, from a mainstream dictionary, is a fairly straightforward, uncontroversial description of the capitalist economic model. How well does any portion of the foregoing definition fit with today's American-led global economy? The initial part of the definition has some basis in fact, although, as stated, much corporate ownership (i.e. the lumber and oil industries) would be impracticable without public complicity. Additionally, the investments that banks and other financial institutions make are overtly affected by the governmental (public) sector, in the form of federal interest rates, bonds, monetary policy, foreign policy (oil, for example), all of which seems somewhat non-capitalist given, "...investments [are supposed to be] determined by private decision." The definition does not say "private decisions based on public monies or monetary policies."

The last part of the definition, i.e. "...competition in a free market," represents the most poignant failure of the U.S. economy to live up to its professed adherence to capitalism. As cited, there exists little in the way of genuine competition considering the public assistance the multinationals rely on for survival. Regardless of this fact, competition, with its implication of many evenly matched competitors, in no way resembles the current reality. Instead what we have are a few massive companies dominating each major industry and these often collude with each other. To call the market under globalization anything akin to "free" is a charade. Thousands of pages have been written just to elucidate the rules pertaining to bi-lateral trade restrictions between the U.S. and other countries, not to mention the number of trade barriers sanctioned by organizations like the World Trade Organization, an outfit ostensibly dedicated to free-market principles.

The "capitalist" economic myth is thus revealed for what it is: an oligarchical, non-competitive, ruling-class economy, dependent on the passive cooperation (through taxation and obedience) of the masses. However, the most ruinous aspect of this particular myth rests not with the existence of a ruling-elite model over a true capitalist model, but with the myth's effect on the average American citizen. Convinced of the general fairness and competition inherent in the commonly understood definition of capitalism and committed to a spectacle orchestrated by the imperial government and the conglomerates, citizens accept outrage after outrage (environmental degradation, nuclear weapons, displacement of jobs, senseless wars, ever increasing income gaps), all in the name of free-market capitalism. The masses, who more often than not believe in American individualism, seldom realize that the passive cooperation they exhibit towards the government is used as a weapon against them, their families and their communities.

GREED AND THE HUMAN CORPORATION

There are, obviously, concrete reasons why multinational corporations are the engine which sow the seeds of global destruction. Some of these have to do with the marriage between like-minded oligarchies, but the biggest governmental boost that corporations ever received was not in the form of tax breaks, subsidies or bailouts, it was the gift of personhood. With a relatively obscure 1886 Supreme Court ruling (*Santa Clara County vs. Southern Pacific Railroad Co.*) the U.S. government conferred individual rights onto all subsequent corporations. This may seem somewhat innocuous or even irrelevant, but it is an essential component of the economy.

By giving human rights to corporations, the Supreme Court made animate an inveterately immoral fabrication. Corporations, similar to the military, are fundamentally immoral because they have one destructive trait that motivates them. In the case of the imperial military, the trait is the urge to dominate and kill, and in the case of the corporation, it is the urge for profit. Neither a pseudo-capitalist nor a member of the ruling-elite would refute this drive for profit at the expense of all else. In fact, one of the commonalities shared by capitalism and globalization is the elevation of human greed to the level of a religious doctrine.

The destruction spawned by the conglomerates finds its life through appealing to humanities' baser instincts. This is not to say that human beings are congenitally greedy, no more than they are congenitally violent, but greed is a human condition, and, as almost every major world religion recognizes, ultimately leads to misery and destroys what is best about humanity. The immorality of greed generally stems from selfishness and the oppression of others.

When comparing greed (selfishness) with compassion (selflessness), one quickly realizes that for any society to function in a healthy way, the latter must outweigh the former. And yet the ruling-elite economy has little room for compassion. This means that in all of the world's societies affected by globalization, people must live a schizophrenic existence in order to be compassionate. In a system that repeatedly denies and devalues such intrinsic human goodness, the populace must see through the fog created by corporate advertisers and media so that social relationships do not dissolve.[vii]

Still, the oppression and exploitation generated by U.S.-led globalization would not be possible if the condition of anthropomorphism was unmet. The immorality, therefore, did not arise solely from the mere presence of globalization. To reach its apex and glory, corporations needed to be recognized as having human rights.[viii] Corporations are not human beings, and their blind lust for wealth (unchecked by a human conscience) makes their immorality inescapable.

NEO-COLONIALISM AS CONSERVATIVE IDEOLOGY

As we compare the economies of the European colonial era to the modern day American neo-colonial era, the similarities stand out far more than the differences, which indicates that globalization is a conservative ideology. Conservative in this case refers primarily to the economy's vested parties, who see no benefit in altering a landscape that has been so favorable to them, albeit in a world beset with constant changes.

Before illuminating the elite's conflicted nature, the harmony of the ruling political parties in the United States needs to again be identified, so that the word "conservative" is not misinterpreted. In the lexicon of American political rhetoric, "conservative" generally means that which is not liberal and vice versa. The ruling parties' desire to cling to their uncomplicated beliefs is explicable. However, anyone who has ever closely observed life recognizes its extreme complexity. While there are tangible rules which apply in the natural world (i.e. a seed is planted and given the right conditions it grows), the overwhelming sensation and marvel of life revolves around constant change which occurs incessantly, trillions and trillions of times, every second, every day. Without evolution, human beings (as one example) would still be living as Neanderthals. In the face of such frightening commotion, the reactionaries cling to their power and money as if it were a life raft that will save them. It is just this adherence to the principles of greed and violence which may eventually be a weak link in their paradigm. And in the face of life's terrifying (for them) uncertainty, may lead to the system failure they desperately fear.

Again, this is no conspiracy theory. The individuals who run the world's prevailing economy have a simple, conservative agenda, with very distinct goals, and as long as money and control comes their way, it does not need to be discussed in secret clubs. Because this perspective so thoroughly dominates American society, it gets sold to citizens in formats ranging from *The New York Times* to public schools. People are told that the market is amoral, that democracy and globalization are one and the same, and that there are no alternative possibilities outside of dictatorships and communism. Yet, this tale, as we have seen, is untrue. Far from being amoral, the market, with greed at its core and military violence as its relief, is patently immoral. Alternate possibilities (to be discussed further in the final chapter) having to do with local, direct democracy do exist, but they exist on a small scale and in the dreams of fanatics.

A WEAPON AGAINST THE POOR

The violence and greed so integral to this economic system do not represent its greatest moral lapses: that distinction belongs to the effect globalization has on the earth's impoverished majority. "Free-market" promoters always wish to point out how much poor countries benefit from globalization.[ix] In very few instances has this proven to be true, and if one looks at the American divide between the rich and poor since the 1970's, the inequality gap expanded tremendously, with the very rich becoming richer and the poor becoming poorer (McMurrer & Sawhill 1998, p. 41-42). Under the neo-colonial regime this phenomenon is common in both developing countries and wealthy countries.

During the post World War II era American empire building quickly accelerated. America pursued a different approach to the developing countries than the Europeans: rather than concentrating on physically conquering lands, U.S. policy makers, under the guise of fighting communism, devised tools such as the

IMF and the World Bank to coerce governments to adopt pro-American economic strategies. The results have been nothing short of disastrous. From dictators stealing loan monies (often leaving tremendous public debts when they are
overthrown or replaced), to displacing centuries-old agricultural communities
in favor of cheap factory labor and agribusiness, to undermining what small public services existed in these countries, to encouraging a financial system that is
permanently damaging the environment (which will ultimately have a much
more severe effect on the world's poorest citizens), neo-colonialist policies have
had a negligible effect in ameliorating world poverty, and in large measure have
made conditions worse. (Weisbrot, et al.)

   And what effect has the more than five decades of failure had on the conservatives' position regarding global wealth inequality? As one would expect,
they persist with their square-peg-in-a-round-hole philosophy, unwilling to
admit that changes, beyond bombing, repression, and increased "security" are
needed. Without the acceptance of the model's failure, there will never be an
end to "terrorism," as the global system daily creates thousands more dispossessed and desperate people.

GLOBALIZATION: DEMOCRACY,
RESISTANCE AND WEAKNESSES

   One of the more persistent myths of American culture is that which links
"capitalism," or, more accurately, globalization, with democracy. This myth pervades the propaganda of the modern-day conservatives who wish to create still
more vassals for their unjust economic cartel. There are numerous reasons why
this perspective is simply not valid, but the myth's underpinning lie relates to the
disparate motives of democracy and imperialism. Just as globalization and its
advocates desire nothing more than economic stagnation (systemic stagnation,
not to be confused with stagnation of profits or growth), true democracy is a
constantly evolving expression of the public will, and even the faux American
democracy represents an antithetical philosophy to globalization. The fact that

our degraded, marginally representative form of government poses a severe threat to globalization finds confirmation in organizations like the World Trade Organization and the North American Free Trade Agreement. Both incarnations are designed, not, as is claimed, to promote free trade, but to buffer the multinationals against the audacity of local democratic control. NAFTA contains rules whereby countries, states or municipalities can be held financially accountable for laws which affect profit. The WTO has similar provisions, allowing member countries to sanction other member countries whose environmental laws (generally passed by representative governments) are deemed barriers to "free trade." These are only two examples of globalization's institutional contempt for and antagonism towards democracy. However, they do reveal such organizations' role, which is to codify, consolidate and brace the multinational neo-colonialists against the peoples' will.

We must revisit the reference to one of globalization's weakest links. Unquestionably, its beneficiaries have, as part of their temper, constructed historically unrivaled pantheons of money, power and privilege. It is this strength, this simplemindedness, this marriage of avarice and aggression that is globalization's weakness. Because humans have not fully fallen for the prescription, and because humanity, in its heart, supports the dispossessed, the mass of people in the world, including those in the developed countries, can at least sense globalization's immorality. Which leads to the current level of global resistance to this system and helps explain why people are beginning to exploit its weaknesses, and why the opposition movement is growing. These weaknesses emanate from the oligarchy's seeming omnipotence. A huge, omnivorous dinosaur, this economic system does not respond well to change, or to human ingenuity (excepting that applied for profit or violence). Yet humanity, like all of nature, is always evolving, and in the case of neo-colonialism, often in ways unfriendly to the regime. In other words, we can see the progression of slavery to serfdom, to colonialism, to neo-colonialism, and we can observe a corresponding evolution of humanity to assert its rights for justice, freedom, morality and real democracy.

The irony of the above assertion is that globalization apologists like Thomas Friedman (Friedman, 2000), credit the market economy for creating conditions whereby humanity may dream of true freedom. Friedman and similar adherents credit the market with positive human attributes, such as adaptability and the ability to foster and cope with evolution.[x] It must be obvious too that anyone who promotes globalization as immutable and beyond human control is also touting a conservative ideology. These backward-looking positions give merit where none is due. Globalization plays the same role as the U.S. Constitution, establishing a set of rules intent on buffering the affluent few against the human aspirations of the impoverished majority.

Another recurring yet faulty argument of globalization's cheerleaders relates to claims that with its constant "evolution" and massive movement of capital, globalization somehow undermines empires and nation states. For a countervailing opinion on this line of reasoning, please see the entirety of this book, which outlines, in part, the incredible amount of power accumulated by the American government and its client states.

One final rebuttal to the apologist's equation of globalization and freedom: globalization and its representatives are in love with authority. The entire system, backed as it is by colossal violence and unaccountable global organizations, represents an ode to authoritarianism, and few could argue that authority and freedom bear any sympathy for each other.

IN TOTO

Now that we have analyzed the corporate monolith and some of its consequences, drawing a few conclusions about globalization proves to be straightforward. My summation consists of two different, interconnected parts. The first concerns the corporate-led economy and where it is inevitably leading humanity -should it remain in control- the second has to do with what may follow once the inevitabilities are broached.

We must first consider the environmental revolt that could take place before or simultaneously with any human revolt. The environmental revolt, which has already begun, is due to an economy predicated on endless growth on a planet with limited resources. When we look at the equation in this manner, we are able to witness a deeply rooted logical absurdity. If the corporate economist knows on a conscious level that earth has finite resources, but finds himself searching for endless economic "growth" through the exploitation of said limited resources, then certainly he must be able to see the writing on the wall. The elite are largely silent on this simple and potent conundrum of globalization. Perhaps the reason one fails to hear this obvious logical disconnect discussed by globalization's proponents rests on the fact that they instinctively know where we are headed and are merely capitalizing and exploiting while they can sustain the veil of denial. Essentially, they are robbing the store before it burns to the ground.

There are other factors that will hasten globalization's decline. Much as it depends on the exploitation of resources, it relies similarly on the exploitation of humanity. This exploitation cuts in disparate directions. On one hand, people become desperate as their cultures are destroyed, both as a result of globalization's natural tendency to dehumanize people (i.e. the will of profit dominating the will of humanity) and as a result of the poor fighting the poorer over scarce resources. On the other hand people suffer (as members of the natural order) from the environmental degradation spawned by corporations. Any or all of these factors may start rebellions or speed-up societal implosion.

I mention rebellion because the eventual reaction to globalization, whether it is human or environmental, promises to be climactic. We know the system will not change of its own accord. As discussed, globalization represents a 500-year-old economic arrangement, which was spawned by earlier versions of European feudalism. It would be ludicrous to expect those who derive enormous material benefits from this order to gracefully lay aside their power, comfort and profits and reform such an entrenched, immoral[xi] economy. But in the end, all of this hoarded power will not be able to stop globalization's demise: it will either implode or be toppled.

Class issues surrounding the perpetuation of globalization deserve mentioning. Other than ruling-elite class behavior, and a passing description of the myth whereby the classes under the ruling-elite tend to view the United States as a classless society, class issues have not been explored here in depth. Although propaganda of a classless United States leads people to believe in a fundamentally untrue myth, it represents only part of the class dilemma. This denial concerning the existence of class finds the overwhelming majority of Americans -those outside the ruling-elite- generally feel comfortable only in institutions which mimic the hierarchical, authoritarian structure of corporations and the government. While this could be seen as yet another propaganda success, the point here is that few Americans have any interest in, or knowledge of alternative means of organization (i.e. non-hierarchical, non-authoritarian). This is ironic given that the benefits of the corporate system are doled out so inequitably. Which brings us to an even larger aid to corporate control. Namely, that America, despite the tremendous amount of money and power held by the very few, is a wealthy nation. What this means is that millions of middle class citizens live lives of material comfort. In fact, the United States possesses the largest middle class in the history of human society.

With such a bounty in place it would seem we have reached a powerful argument against the allegations in this chapter and in favor of a ruling-elite, corporate-controlled economy. Weighing its obvious negative consequences for both humanity and the environment, one could argue that it provides, at the very least, material well being for millions of people. What could possibly be wrong with this, especially considering the destitution experienced by the majority of the earth's inhabitants?

The response is intimately related to said destitution and to the essence of slavery or freedom. By willingly participating in, supporting and venerating globalization, the American middle classes play a most crucial role in the machine. As underlings in an elite economy, they act, regardless of their job titles, as one large service industry. Or, seen differently, the middle classes are a bit like southern slaves who were given "forty acres and a mule" following the American Civil War (in this case, televisions, cars, and a ranch house). They are living in a system designed to make sure they stay in their place.

Thus as members of the middle class live their lives of material well-being, they are, from the elite perspective, tools to be used as befits the economy. And if the middle class is just that, an instrument to promote the corporate order's immoral dictates, then, stupor notwithstanding, they too are culpable for its actions. If this master and puppet analogy feels forced or contrived, observe how the average middle-class American lives and follow the money trail. People in this group purchase gas produced by any number of oil conglomerates. They have retirement investments in companies on the stock market that are concerned with making a profit at the expense of all else. They have mortgages with banks interested only in exploitation though interest collection. They buy their food from agribusinesses, distributed via multinational chain stores that are destroying the soil (the basis of human life), entire ecosystems, and agricultural communities. They buy their drugs from companies that focus on wealth rather than wellness. They provide taxes so that the Pentagon can continue its march of imperialism. All this for what? Peoples' desires and needs may be partially satisfied by these actions, but their assigned function remains to service the elite. Globalization is a game designed to have one set of winners; everyone else gets left with the scraps. Middle class Americans (Europeans, etc.) receive sufficient material goods for their obedience, and the rest of the world's population receives indigence with empty promises of future material benefits.

Where does any hope lie, given the existing parameters? With the U.S.-led military and corporate entities having their way with the world, the developed world's middle classes apathetic and cowed by their goods, and the developed and undeveloped world's poor suffering to the point of an economically-sanctioned death, this would appear to be a hopeless situation. And yet we know that the present arrangement sows the seeds of its eventual destruction. We also know that not all of the underlings are cowed or disenfranchised. They are beginning to resist in large numbers (see any number of the worldwide anti-globalization protests, or the overwhelming global opposition to the current U.S. war on Iraq). Of these knowable realities, the resistance offers human beings one path to follow amidst the oppression.

The timeline for globalization's demise cannot easily be measured, but individual and group opposition can be. No path will be devoid of suffering, but positive rebelliousness and insubordination provide for some measure of optimism. Perhaps courage, which gives people strength to resist the irresistible, will, in the end, triumph over fear, violence and greed.

6

OLIGARCHY, APATHY AND RESISTANCE

"We are moving into a new latitude of the soul,
and a thousand years hence men will wonder at our blindness,
our torpor, our supine acquiescence to an order which was doomed."

– HENRY MILLER
The Colossus of Maroussi

"Each of us inevitable,
Each of us limitless-each of us with his or her right upon the earth,
Each of us allow'd the eternal purports of the earth,
Each of us here as divinely as any is here."

– WALT WHITMAN
Salute Au Monde!

"Therefore soldiers are most invincible when they will not conquer.
When a tree is grown to its greatest strength it is doomed.
The strong and the great stay below; the tender and the weak rise above."

– LAO TSE

While this final chapter may in part serve as a conclusion, touching on many of the themes and ideas of the previous chapters, it will not be an attempt to sum up the book's entirety. Instead, I will turn to the themes of oligarchy, apathy and resistance to conclude my observations on American imperialism. These three concepts are effective barometers as to the state of the Empire, although it is my opinion that all of the writing up to this point describes, in some manner, the American imperial dilemma.

This chapter will also differ from the others by suggesting tangible actions that can and are being taken to resist the Empire's vagaries. Ideas surrounding resisting monolithic power are likely to appeal to Americans' empathy for the underdog and should resonate with our humanness. Resistance to imperialism represents a form of courage and divinity. And while divinity is intrinsic to the human condition, it is, more importantly, antithetical to the characteristics of empire.

As discussed earlier, the Cold War conflict between the United States and the Soviet Union had less to do with ideology than with competition between two oligarchical empires over control of global resources. Under the guise of capitalism and communism, the leaders of these states acquired as much power, money and resources as possible. As a rule, states that become empires will operate as oligarchies. All empires are ruled by a relative few with the leaders aiming to accumulate colossal levels of power and wealth. Many would argue that America exemplifies the exception to that rule, being the first empire in history to function as some form of democracy. However, if one takes a close look at the organization of the United States, it quickly becomes clear that oligarchy rules the day.

In American society, the three controlling entities -the state, corporations and the military- all predictably exhibit oligarchical temperaments. The focus in this chapter on corporations and the state (the oligarchical nature of any military system being a given) is an effort to recognize America as an empire with oligarchy as its core operating principle. The corporation's and the state's hierarchical structure not only define the overall mindset of American society -with masses of people willing to accept illegitimate authority as an unalterable reality- they undermine democracy, commodify life and strive for nothing less than the acquiescence of the entire populace.

STATE OLIGARCHY

First we must take a broad view of what role the nation-state plays in human society. States at their most basic level are human groupings based on culture, geography, religion and history, run by some sort of governing body or ruling authority. Nation-states obviously range in size from very small to very large.

Within this range one may find a tiny state that runs in an oligarchical fashion, or a larger state that operates in a more democratic manner. But, with such possibilities noted, there exists a strong historical connection between large states or empires and oligarchical, undemocratic ruling authorities. Without belaboring a point made in previous chapters, empires from the Egyptian to the British were modeled on a hierarchical ruling structure.[i]

It would be quite difficult to argue that the impoverished, disenfranchised members of imperial oligarchies benefited much from their compliance, and there is little doubt that the marble palaces, pyramids, etc. built for the ruling class represent the rewards of their dominance. Such benefits are gained not just through proletariat subservience, but also through the threat and application of internal and external violence.

Are we then to assume that all states are inherently violent? And, by extension, are empires violent relative to their size? These questions lead to contradictory answers. On the one side, we can observe that under the present system of human organization (with nation-states ruling the planet) the majority of people live their lives without experiencing daily violence.[ii] Conversely, the violence perpetrated by nations has persisted unabated from earliest recorded history to the nuclear-armed 21st century. What this apparently paradoxical situation tells us has more to do with the complexity of humanity than the inevitability of our present condition. Humans have the ability to be both violent and non-violent, with the non-violent side being the more predominant and moral impulse. In the era of recorded history, mass violence (war) manifests itself as a condition of the state, and the larger the state, generally the larger the war machine. Thus a key role of state oligarchies is to encourage humanity to debase itself via concerted violence for the charity of the elite.

If we accept that non-violence represents the moral or divine in humanity, then alternatively we can assume that although violence is a part of the human reality, it represents a weakness and degrades our lives on earth. Additionally, state-sponsored violence clearly inhibits evolution, and indicates an absence of vision, a void of wisdom, and a fear of positive change. Oligarchic states require the citizenry to subvert their own divinity in favor of a state morality, which is professed, but, due to states' inherent immorality, cannot exist.

Inevitably, state oligarchies tend to threaten almost everything that we as a species need or hold sacred. These threats include (but are not limited to): a contempt and hostility for human rights, an avaricious and destructive relationship with the natural world, the glorification of militarism, and an aversion to truly democratic human organization. This final characteristic is interesting to note within the context of America's democratic myth. If one deliberates on the logistics of human organization it becomes obvious that for people in a society to partake in decision-making and to feel invested in that process, numbers above a few hundred participants make true democracy unfeasible. Real democracy and small numbers of people are as inseparable as oligarchy is to empire.

Even though the multitude of democracy mountebanks (the mainstream media, the government, large corporations) in the United States would have people believe otherwise, the country has all of the aforementioned attributes of an oligarchy and few of a democracy. On a strictly practical level it is simply impossible for the 500 or so elected national representatives (representing two barely distinguishable political parties) to democratically represent the will of 300 million people.[iii]

Still, democracy does rear its head in America, partially in spite of the ruling authorities and partially because of them. This democratic rebellion has been an ongoing phenomenon throughout American history, driving humanity forward, accepting evolution and change as necessary, desirable and enlightened. The changes occurred and continue to occur whenever individuals unite in organized resistance to the policies of the privileged. It can be as small as a citizens' meeting or as large as the civil rights movement. Whatever the case, by eroding the elite power base, people have succeeded in making America resemble a democracy from time to time. But this is almost always due to agitation from the bottom up, with immutable governmental leaders resisting human evolution until their hands are forced. One unpleasant outcome for the leaders who constantly extol democracy is that some citizens actually end up believing and acting as if they live in a democracy. Perhaps America's authorities should be excused for this failure as every method of crowd control has some drawbacks.

CORPORATE OLIGARCHY

In modern American society, the only institutions to rival the state and the military for influence are corporations. [iv] Similar to the nature of large states, all large corporations exhibit oligarchical behavior, and these multinational businesses display as much contempt for democracy as empires do. In fact, it is the confluence of interests between the American Empire and large corporations which creates such a deadly combination for humanity. The ramifications produced by the existence of these monoliths, for militarism, the environment, human rights, etc. are analogous to those caused by imperialism. And although the long arm of state propaganda infuses almost every aspect of life in American society, the propaganda forwarded by the oligarchical corporate behemoths match the best efforts of the government.

What the organizational structure of oligarchy provides corporations, above all else, is a narrowness of opinion. With the limited number of people in control of these entities as compared to the millions they employ as workers (not to mention the hundreds of millions more who are affected by their policies), decision-making falls under a very partial review, which, to the credit of oligarchy, is an efficient way to formulate policy. Unfortunately, to a person, these CEOs, presidents, CFOs, etc. all have but one thing in mind when reaching any decisions: profit. Therefore, when labor begins to organize in a particular retail store then it is shut down (see Wal-Mart); if thousands are poisoned and killed in India due to malfeasance, efforts are made to keep the incident under wraps and leave quickly (see Union Carbide); if a company produces low-grade nuclear devices which have sickened thousands of its own country's military personnel, the news is kept out of the yearly business report (see Starmet); if the cost of energy is artificially inflated to make billions, at the expense of customers and employees, the auditors simply "cook the books" (see Enron and Arthur Anderson). These types of decisions are not exceptional. They are the kind routinely made by the captains of industry.

No matter how much lip service gets paid to "keeping the consumer's interests first" or how much money is given to charity by the Gates Foundation, everything comes down to profit in the eyes of the oligarch. It may be because corporations' paths are guided by the limited worldviews of a few people that more equitable human groupings do not materialize.[v] Nevertheless, the failure of corporate oligarchy to respond to the earth's deepening environmental and human crises demonstrates that this form of organization is not sustainable and will ultimately perpetrate, through a lack of foresight, its own demise.

Oligarchies stifle and detest true competition. Take a look at any key global industry and you will find oligarchy, not competition. Whether it be cars, communications, airplanes, travel, entertainment, there are seldom more than a half dozen serious players and often fewer than that. And if one looks for a variety of economic opinions on news reports, for a variance of prices between "competing" gas stations located next to each other, or for affordable health insurers, you quickly recognize that serious alternatives do not exist. And the reason they do not exist rests on the fact that oligarchies, by nature, would rather collude than compete.

Large states love these corporations because they speak the same language of concentrated wealth and power, and vice versa. The state can contract with the oligarchies to provide the things it needs for it own furtherance, like nuclear weapons, propaganda masquerading as news, etc. So too for the corporations, which use their power to curry favor with politicians, use the government as a medium for taxpayers to fund their products and research (while avoiding and lobbying against their own taxes), use the American military to open up overseas markets, and use the state to create rules (NAFTA, FTAA, WTO) which assist and protect their operations. Other than providing their tax dollars, small American businesses (just like the majority of American citizens) have no say in this exchange. The state and business oligarchs speak a dialect of mutual benefit, whose words are coded for consensual satisfaction.

The lie that uncompetitive, neo-capitalistic oligarchy is the only viable method for organizing humanity must be refuted for its utter falseness. It's absurd to believe that the world's poor (who represent the vast majority of the world's populace) support an economic regime whereby individuals like Bill Gates hold wealth greater than the sum of many nations. "Competitive" and "capitalism" do not apply as words with specific meanings to corporate-led, state-supported globalization. We must remember that capitalism means, specifically, "...competition in a free market." Who but the wealthiest individuals and corporations could "compete" in the current climate?

The great irony of the American state preaching liberty and democracy to its charges, while functioning in an antithetical manner, applies as well to the multinational corporation. Rather than attempting to foster patriotism or an allegiance to the state (although this does occur), corporations commonly advertise their products as helping people realize freedom, independence, liberty, and individualism. The positive spin on this reality is that Americans obviously have a deep affinity for these democratic ideals, otherwise they would not respond to such tactics. Corporate advertisers employ propaganda techniques (similar to those of the state) to achieve loyalty among "consumers," essentially marketing people's enslavement under the guise of freedom.

The malfeasance of corporate oligarchy does not end with advertising. So many U.S. citizens have their money invested in the stock market, banks, bonds and mutual funds, that even though the owners of capital still run and control the economy, the average middle class person has a real affinity for this system of global exploitation. And who could blame them for feeling this way? The myth claims that a person just needs to invest "wisely" and by retirement age they should have enough cash to live out a comfortable life of leisure. Of course things do not often work out this way (especially when elderly health care expenses are factored in), and the whole scheme is based on unearned, speculative income: a Ponzi scheme on a grand scale.

To put it more succinctly, the individual who relies upon unearned income (interest) falls prey to two different conundrums. The first is that small-time stock market players with a middle class income or lower have no guarantees of any return on their "investment." Their chosen company, the stock market, their IRA, or their mutual fund could collapse overnight and they would be left with nothing. They simply provide the liquid assets that feed the market. When a person relies upon speculative income, this is the chance he or she takes. The rich, however, are seldom adversely affected by market swings because the market was designed by the wealthy. So the conundrum is that alongside deceitful advertisements to sell products, the stock market and other forms of speculative income -which sustain the oligarchy- offer the layperson what amounts to a seemingly effortless, yet frequently illusionary pot of gold. The second problem rests on the morality of supporting, through speculative investments, a system that injuriously exploits countrymen and foreigners alike, simply for avarice. We must not deceive ourselves. While the game is designed and dominated by the rich, the billions of dollars contributed in small sums by millions of dispensable "investors" adds up to a very indispensable sum of money.

An argument made by many is that the American legal system buffers the middle class against the impulses of the corporate ruling class. Unlike a country run by a confirmed dictatorship, where laws evolve to satisfy the ruler's urges and kangaroo courts prevail, America has a comparatively developed legal system. So in a very real sense, the U.S. Empire internally is a less repressive regime than a dictatorship.[vi] The laws in place to enforce the oligarchy do trickle down in the form of elements such as due process, trial by jury, Miranda rights, innocent until proven guilty, etc. However, this should not be viewed as an out for those who would see in the American legal system a safeguard against the depredations of oligarchy. The primary fault of this particular line of defense rests in the fact that the majority of American laws were and are written by the ruling classes to satisfy elite concerns. Laws (beyond those prohibiting murder, rape, etc.) are simply one group's (the elite) effort to legitimize and codify particular behaviors, and to then back them up with the threat of violence (the police) or incarceration. From criminal law to corporate law, the deck is stacked against the disenfranchised. And if the laws in place are not enough to satisfy the oligarchy's desires, then they are fine-tuned, or completely rewritten as needed.[vii] Thus, one could make the argument that whatever protections the average citizen receives from legislation are merely by-products, with the true purpose of the whole legal apparatus being to service the oligarchy.

One last note on corporate oligarchy: a factor that distinguishes the American oligarchy from other historical oligarchies is modern communication. The tools of modern communication (television, radio, newsprint, magazines, the internet, etc.) are largely controlled by multinational corporations whose primary goal is to extend their hegemony and profits. They are succeeding fabulously. In fact, their success has led to a worldwide cultural commodification, which distorts, to the advantage of the oligarchy, the perspective of the billions who ingest their "information products." The word "product" describes everything the communications companies sell. If pundits are discussing a potential war, it is not debated it is sold. Advertisements for laundry detergent fill the spaces between the news pitches, thereby creating a closed loop, with wars, famine, murder, cars, and entertainment all designed for the purpose of promoting corporate greed. Commodifying life simplifies the world for easy digestion and transforms everything into diversion, advertisements, or both ideally. Viewed from this perspective, the masses are consumers, not individuals, and the media corporations' actions stem from this requisite principle. In the history of humanity, no oligarchical authority has ever had this level of power and influence over propaganda and myth.

APATHY AND INDOCTRINATION

With the worldwide control of information resources at the disposal of corporate giants, it is no wonder the level of political apathy within the American populace is at an all time high.

Still, arguments pertaining to issues of apathy or indoctrination are tricky to navigate because they involve chicken and egg scenarios. According to standard right-wing ideology, people determine their own destinies irrespective of outside inputs. This means that even if an individual gets inundated with external messages from birth to death, their actions and reactions to these messages are his or her responsibility alone. Those on the left generally argue the reverse, that people, regardless of their best efforts, cannot help but be molded by external forces. The left puts a heavy faith in propaganda, be it pro-oligarchy (seen as negative), or anti-oligarchy (seen as positive). Because there are external forces which undeniably affect an individual's level of apathy, and because there are also internal forces which can help a person resist such obfuscation, both perspectives must be given some credence. The following short dissection of indoctrination and apathy will be a mutation of these ostensibly divergent political philosophies. The power of individual conscience may represent the crossroads of these two perceptions.

A number of factors need attention in any study pertaining to the effect of indoctrination upon the mass of U.S. citizens. One must look at the structure and content of education (both public and private), the configuration and bias of media and information sources, the legal system, and the overarching cultural orientation of a society in order to ascertain the external factors which contribute to passivity. Although many of these issues have been referenced in the preceding pages, the aim here is to unify them into a more pointed exploration.

THE INDOCTRINATING ROLE OF EDUCATION

Any cursory survey of the American public education complex reveals its glaring inadequacies. Perhaps there is not a political issue in the United States on which more people agree. And although there is consensus that problems exist, what is wrong with schools and how to fix them is cause for endless debate. Problems like crime and dilapidated buildings in inner city schools (compared with video studios, relative safety and posh buildings in nearby suburban schools) offer a powerful indictment of U.S. public education (and our society as a whole). But, to some degree, they are what one would expect to find in an imperial society.[viii]

The corruption of youth through the American educational juggernaut goes deeper than simply modeling societal failures. While the school system is modeled after the hierarchy, injustice and immorality of the larger empire, the most damning disservice done to U.S. children is the content of their education.

It must be said that within the enormous realm of public education there obviously exists an incredibly wide spectrum of teachers, teaching methods and subject matter. Even so, there is perhaps no greater, more concentrated level of mass indoctrination than in American public schools. While the U.S. elites may not all share the same philosophy around public education, the majority fully back the concept of schools reinforcing the idea that education should enhance a child's respect for the state and our schools perform this task better than any other institution. From saluting the flag at the beginning of every day, to worshipping sports and athletes, to the forced daily regimentation (replete with ringing bells signaling release and lockdown), to social sciences based on lies and myths, the average school prepares the average student for a life of mediocrity and submission to an unmistakably immoral sociopolitical order. In the eyes of the authorities, the submission of individual conscience to the will of the state is the most invaluable lesson a student can learn.

The indoctrination of students manifests itself in other ways as well. Before pupils graduate from high school they are tracked into different categories based on their economic class. Working class and lower class students generally get funneled into vocational type training, while middle and upper middle class kids (the upper classes typically send their children to elite private schools) are directed toward a "college prep" course of study. This accomplishes two state-approved goals. It helps to ensconce and legitimize the American class structure and provides subservient workers for blue and white-collar professions.

As American children grow older the media's role as indoctrinator gradually replaces the educational system as the primary vehicle for championing the supremacy of the state. Short of fully reiterating points already made, the mass media plays an important role in supporting and fulfilling the Empire's needs. This role of the media as a tool of the state is not, as we have seen, a one-way relationship. The American media benefits tremendously from its cozy fraternity with the Empire, and the Empire derives an even larger benefit in terms of mass indoctrination.

THE MEDIA AS IMPERIAL CHEERLEADER

People who revel in the idea of the American "free" press would recoil at the above description of the media as an establishment device. These same individuals would point to the daily parade of criticism leveled at the U.S. government by the mainstream media as evidence of press freedom. The question here is not if the media ever criticizes the government, but rather the nature of their cardinal philosophy vis-à-vis the American state. As we explored in the "liberal" *New York Times'* coverage of the Gulf War, no mainstream media outlet with any drive towards selling advertisements, or receiving preferential treatment from government officials, would dare cast serious aspersions against the defining mantras of U.S. imperialism.

During the cold war, propagandists in the United States used Soviet newspapers like Pravda to their advantage by pointing out that these media outlets' subordination to the state indicated the absence of a free press, and thus the presence of a totalitarian society. But where does the corporate media in America live up to its role as a bastion of freedom? Mainstream U.S. news organizations may criticize their own government, but they are all, by design and necessity, subservient to the state. Evidence that fault can be placed on the mainstream media is found in non-commercial (i.e. non-dependent) American media entities. Because it is non-commercial, the independent media is more legitimately free than any corporate media, free from bowing to advertisers and free from bowing to the state.[ix] Independent media outlets are also free to dissect the values and motivations of U.S. imperialism, and they do so, proving that organizations can simultaneously exist in an empire and deliberate over its reason for being.

THE LEGAL SYSTEM AND INDOCTRINATION

If one were to focus exclusively on the Supreme Court, it would take thousands of pages to analyze its supporting role in the American Empire. The same holds true in analyzing the role the legal system as a whole plays in mass indoctrination. Rather than zeroing in on American's obsession with the law, or the fact that the country is largely run by lawyers who clog the halls of Congress, this short critique will aim to demonstrate how ruling-elite legality is promoted as beneficial for society and the corollary idea that the state, as the paternal enforcer of these laws, must also be beneficial.

The concept of the United States being, before all else, a nation of laws, is one of the most repeated pieces of information imparted to America's youth. Beginning with the Constitution's glorious ascendancy over the "chaotic" Articles of Confederation, the student is told to look upon the laws of the United States as sacred. This extreme bias regaling the beauty of the American system of law would have students erroneously believe that the Constitution was divinely inspired holy writ.

Beyond this indoctrination on the history of U.S. law, citizens are given their legal parameters through laws passed by "elected" representatives. There are a couple of immediately apparent inconsistencies with this particular setup. The first is the inherent paternalism of having a nominally elected[x] federal politician theoretically speak for hundreds of thousands of people. Assuming that laws, (once again excluding universal crimes like rape, murder, etc.) are based on community values and ethics, how could one person act as a judge for hundreds of communities? The only way this can be realized is through the representative's authoritarian instincts, wherein they believe they have the prescience to comprehend a tremendously diverse group of needs. Therefore this paternalistic lawmaking, instead of being directed by local community needs, is generally informed by the needs of the Empire, the needs of multinational corporations, or both. The second inconsistency has to do with an immoral state determining laws based on morality. States, especially empires, are the biggest lawbreakers imaginable, and they tend to violate laws that we as humans consider to be intrinsically correct. Murder, illegal nationwide, is promoted and sanctioned (via America's omnipotent war apparatus) as a normal and healthy part of the Empire. What's more, although murder is illegal in all U.S. states, many of them "legally" execute those convicted of committing murder. The list of laws perpetrated and enforced by the American state that are objectionable in their own right (regardless of the irrationality of immoral states passing moral laws) is quite impressive. (For a partial inventory of these flagrant affronts please see endnotes 6 and 7 for this chapter.)

People have consciences but states do not. And this is a key reason why so much hypocrisy exists within the U.S. legal system. An empire is as blind to justice as it is to injustice. So while the push (through assorted channels of indoctrination) for the masses to believe in the state's beneficence continues unabated, the prospect of an empire as a just arbiter of law should, with the slightest amount of moral scrutiny, be viewed as an impossibility.

CULTURAL IMPERATIVES, ILLUSION AND APATHY

There are broad cultural imperatives in the United States, encouraged by governmental authorities, advertisers, educators, the law and the mass media that play a role in the public's indoctrination and apathy. In this instance I am referring to the illusionary sense of these imperatives, i.e. standard cultural directives that are ultimately based on fallacies. Often these illusions cause a tremendous amount of damage. To clarify, the foregoing description has to do with culturally dominant perceptions. There are abundant examples of opposite modes of behavior within the United States.

Countless external forces contribute to passivity and culturally prescribed illusions fall under this heading. Many of these illusions have been referred to in earlier chapters, albeit in different contexts. The current ruling-elite economy is based on having a docile group of respectfully obedient consumers at its disposal. This obedience is partially achieved by tapping into the illusion of individual salvation through materialism; the paradigm in which functioning as a consumer is equated with happiness.[xi] The average U.S. consumer may realize a temporal happiness or fleeting alleviation of discomfort through mindless expenditures, but corporations and the government almost always benefit. Just as individuals will in the end suffer under the auspices of excessive consumption, globalization thrives. This is because the two entities have very divergent needs, with the ruling-elite economy being a perpetually unsatisfied, multi-headed animal. The individual human, in contrast, is a creature of nature, needing emotional and spiritual wealth. To put it another way, humanity is connected to the divine, new cars, television sets and Coke are not.

Americans are instructed from an early age to believe in the sanctity of empire (disguised as a democracy). We are told in numerous ways that there is redemption in spreading the American dream throughout the entire world. This is an illusion as well because faith in any state, let alone a predatory empire, is antithetical to humanity's spiritual nature. With the Empire's mantras being violence, greed, and repression, and with human beings needing love, compassion, freedom and cooperation to healthily survive on the planet, there exists a complete disconnect between what we are told and what is valid. We must admit that the former attributes are alive in the human world, but they are all inexorably destructive traits. And if followed as a path to deliverance, they lead directly to unnecessary suffering, inhumane hierarchy and societal collapse.

In analyzing these external factors that constitute some of the indoctrination methods employed by the authorities and by the culture, we have not delved into what makes a person or a society politically apathetic. Apathy, unlike external efforts of indoctrination, is more difficult to measure because it is largely an internal process. So while we can attribute at least a share of America's mass passivity to indoctrination, facets of the process will forever be a mystery. There is a tangible negative relationship between larger human groupings and democracy. There is also a relationship between the size of a state and the will of people to participate. An individual's level of apathy seems to increase in proportion to the scale of the institution of which they are a part.

Although we cannot fully comprehend what makes a person passive, we are able to witness the conflict it engenders. Note the detachment needed for the Washington D.C. tourist industry to thrive. As middle class tourists walk around the city they are continually confronted with destitute people. Given the disparity of wealth people witness when they juxtapose D.C.'s abject poverty with its gleaming federal buildings, there is no doubt that thousands of Washington tourists experience a profound spiritual discomfort during their visit. And while they may not want to attribute their discomfort to any particular cause, they are, in essence, having a human reaction to byproducts of the inhumane Empire.

MORAL RESISTANCE

Relative to its number of citizens, the incidence of people in the United States exercising their civil liberties in the form of protesting, dissidence and organizing is fairly low. One could attribute this situation to any number of factors, from television, to indoctrination, to a large materially satiated middle-class. But, resistance does endure and has since America's inception. In view of the multiple indictments of American society and imperialism contained in this book, the scope of the problems presented by the United States' existence would seem to be desperate beyond measure. However, this is precisely why a short discourse on moral resistance, as an antidote to the excesses of empire, concludes this final chapter.

We have repeatedly witnessed the American Empire's narrowly prescribed impulses. Such impulses prevent the state from adapting well to change, something that individuals, with the will, can do. Everything about the United States power structure conjures images of an enormous, bloated dinosaur incapable of turning around enough to see its own tail. And this characteristic, in terms of resistance, is of paramount value. As the Daoists understood, anything so large and so powerful must unavoidably possess correspondingly immense weaknesses. And these weaknesses are what millions of people in the United States and abroad are attempting to exploit.

Before exploring moral actions that are, or can be, taken to resist the Empire, a word needs to be said about violence. In any resistance, revolution or rebellion, debates always arise as to whether or not violence should be employed to achieve dissidents' goals. The opinion here is that belligerence by humans against other humans typically leads to an ever-escalating cycle of violence and tends to degrade humanity as a whole.[xii] If we are to ever realize our potential as a species, it will not be through the use of violent force.

Continuing on in this vein, any moral resistance should be rooted in some core of spiritual awareness, even if it is as simple as empathizing with human frailties and the struggle for humane social relations. To phrase it differently, men and woman of numerous organized religions could find endless reasons, within the constructs of their respective faiths, to resist the current order. In the case of Christianity, one has to distinguish between the charlatans who run the country, and Christians who follow literally the teachings of Christ. This is because (particularly when right-wing evangelists preach Christianity and patriotism as one and the same) church leaders often end up acting as sycophants for the state, and thus work against Christ's message of love, harmony and forgiveness.

What are people doing at the present time to resist U.S.-led imperialism, globalization and militarism? The forms resistance takes are as innumerable as the inspired individuals and groups who initiate them. Any list pertaining to methods of dissent must be seen as a partial one only. The following are examples that have proven effective in some way. All of the ensuing behaviors are a fruitful response to the present world order and people are encouraged to try any or all of these for themselves. It can be a deeply liberating experience.

Public protest is an important element of moral resistance. This is perhaps the most effective political tool for activists, not because it changes the minds of the elite,[xiii] but because it is a genuine form of personal political expression (as opposed to voting, which in the Empire amounts to an endorsement of preordained policies). For Americans, protest represents the reverse of the conformist's tendency to be silent and apathetic. There are so many reasons (and methods) for protesting in the United States that if a person listens to his or her conscience long enough, he or she will discover what needs to be done.

Another positive approach to resistance is to organize. Cooperatives, political groups, unions and alternative media outlets are a few possible approaches. It is best to seek out organizations of like-minded humans, in small groups that are non-hierarchical, respect peoples' individuality and refuse to copy imperial systems. This step is more difficult than the first because it involves compromise and cooperation, two attributes that are not commonly modeled for most U.S. citizens. Even though groups are thornier to navigate than individual action, they are essential tools in resisting the Empire, due both to strength in numbers (within limits), and to the solidarity provided by other people under what can be trying circumstances.

One notable form of resistance to the Empire is to be a war tax resister. This form of resistance is listed after the previous two not because it is less relevant or important, but because it may involve a life of harassment by authorities with a tremendous amount of power at their disposal. War tax resistors can put aside a portion of the money they would have paid towards the military. They can find under the table work. Or, perhaps the most attractive of the three, they can earn so little money as to be below a taxable income. The third choice is the most effectual in that it helps people avoid state harassment (thus freeing up time and energy for other types of resistance), and doubly assists their cause, by not playing the game of materialism, thus subverting the imperial economy. Being a war tax resister may (although not always) lead to a life of suffering at the hands of the state. For those with the will to tolerate these potential calamities, there is no better way to register one's moral opposition to militarism, imperialism and globalization.

With respect to undermining the dominant economy, there are a number of effective ways to do this. Most prominently, moral resistance to U.S. imperialism demands a complete withdrawal from the system of speculative, unearned income. The largest section of the American economy derives its sustenance via interest accumulated through investments in banks, stocks, bonds, mutual funds and other such instruments.[xiv] Masses of middle Americans have come to view this money as an inalienable right, as an easy way to become wealthier, and as a way to guarantee their financial security. Until these profits are recognized for what they are, the lifeblood of the ruling-elite economy, of neo-colonial exploitation of the world's poor, and of environmental degradation, the suffering caused by the U.S. Empire will continue largely unhampered.

Refusing to do business with or purchase anything from multinational corporations is, in its own small way, revolutionary. It is a refusal to contribute to injustice, or better still, is like reallocating money from the rich to the poor. If items are needed that are made only by multinationals then a person could buy them secondhand. Using secondhand goods is far better than recycling and helps decrease the waste-stream created by globalization. Other possible acts of insubordination include walking, riding a bike, driving less, taking public transport, buying local food and local products, divesting from the stock market, making compost, reducing meat consumption, using renewable energy, using less energy, growing some food, etc. All of these decisions, while not enough on their own, go a little way towards reducing America's negative impact on the world.[xv] Exhortations of this sort are not original and have been preached a thousand times to the majority. Perhaps this is all the more reason to mention them again.

Living in modern day American society need not be limited to acts of political defiance and rebellion. Individuals and groups can create valuable lives in ways that are antithetical to imperial needs. One way to achieve this goal is to focus on the most local arena, the household economy. By incorporating at least some facet of subsistence through the home, people acquire freedom from the state.[xvi] Whether this means educating children, growing vegetables, building a home from local, renewable materials, or producing goods for sale or barter, emancipation starts at home. From this point, people need to look no further than their immediate surroundings to create (or join) social institutions that undermine blind state authority by focusing on local, cooperative, egalitarian, mutually beneficial human relationships. While voting for Democrats and Republicans only reinforces the Empire's democratic charade, participating in local decision-making (provided the institutions are not those which mimic ruling-elite models) can provide a powerful antidote to the stultification of apathy, conformity and submission. The numerous manifestations of such groups have been hinted at already. Suffice it to say, the options are boundless.

The wonderful thing about such measures, be they local economic units or political organizations, is that although they apply to the present, they will be especially applicable in the future, when the Empire begins to implode.[xvii] During imminent times of state crisis, as the Empire's power weakens or breaks down, it will be the smaller, well-organized communities that will most effectively deal with such upheavals.

If there is doubt that moral resistance has validity, proof can be found. It exists in thousands of examples across the United States and around the world, which are expanding as this is being written.

In a very real way the failings of the United States Empire are both reflective and symbolic of human failures. A primary goal of this book has been to analyze the symbols, human frailties and destructive myths from which the unjust imperial authority derives its license. The hope is that once unfettered from these shackles, people may more objectively view the state and then take action where they deem necessary. It is this existing and potential resistance that represents the best of what American society has to offer.

BIBLIOGRAPHY

CHAPTER 1

A Country Made by War From the Revolution to Vietnam-The Story of America's Rise to Power
Geoffrey Perret 1989 Random House New York, New York

A History of the American People
Paul Johnson 1997 HarperCollins Publishers, Inc. New York, New York

Atomic Audit: The Costs and Consequences of U.S. Nuclear Policy Since 1940
Stephen I. Schwartz 1998 Brookings Institution Press, Washington D.C.

The Beard's New Basic History of the United States
Charles A. and Mary R. Beard 1968 Doubleday and Company, Inc. Garden City, New York

Political and Social History if the United States 1492-1828
Homer C. Hockett 1931 The Macmillan Co. New York, New York

The Reconstruction of American History
John Higham, Ed. 1980 Greenwood Press Publishers, Westport, CT

Main Currents in American Thought from the Beginnings to 1920
Vernon Louis Parrington 1927, 1930 Harcourt, Brace and CO., New York

A Short History of the American People Robert Granville Caldwell 1925, G.P. Putnam's Sons The
Knickerbocker Press, New York & London

The Glorious Cause The American Revolution 1763-1789
Robert Middlekauff 1982, Oxford University Press, New York & Oxford

American Violence A Documentary History
Richard Hofstadter and Michael Wallace, eds. 1970 Alfred A. Knopf, Inc., New York

Free Government in the Making Readings in American Political Thought (2nd Edition)
Alpheus Thomas Mason 1956 Oxford University Press, New York

Perspectives in American History Volume I 1967 Bernard Bailyn and Donald Fleming, eds. 1967
The President and Fellows at Harvard College, Cambridge, Massachusetts

A Different Mirror A History of Multicultural America
Ronald Takaki 1993 Little, Brown and Company, Boston, Toronto, London

The Limits of American Liberty American History 1607-1980 Maldwyn A. Jones 1983 Oxford
University Press, Oxford, New York

Unfree Labor American Slavery and Russian Serfdom Peter Kolchin 1987 The Belknap Press of
Harvard University Press, Cambridge, MA and London

The Free and the Unfree A New History of the United States Peter N. Carroll and David W. Noble 1977 Penguin Books, New York, New York

Free and Independent The Confederation of the United States 1781-1789 Noel B. Gerson 1970 Thomas Nelson, Inc. Camden, New Jersey

The Vineyard of Liberty James MacGregor Burns 1991 Alfred A. Knopf, Inc. New York, New York

A People's History of the United States 1492-Present Howard Zinn 1995 Harper Collins Publishers, Inc. New York, New York

CHAPTER 2

The Cost and Consequences of U.S. Nuclear Weapons Since 1940 Stephen T. Schwartz, ed. 1998 The Brookings Institution Press, Washington D.C.

Mass Culture: The Popular Arts In America B. Rosenberg & D.M. White, eds.1957 New York Free Press, New York, New York

The New Media Monopoly Ben H. Bagdikian 2004 Beacon Press, Boston, Massachusetts

The Divided Welfare State Jacob S. Hacker 2002 Cambridge University Press

Manufacturing Consent The Political Economy of the Mass Media Noam Chomsky and Edward S. Herman 1988 Pantheon Books New York, New York

In China, So Many Liberties, So Little Freedom Erik Eckholm *The New York Times Week in Review* p. 1:10 January 3, 1999

Getting Ahead: Economic and Social Mobility in America Daniel P. McMurrer & Isabel V. Sawhill, eds. 1998 The Urban Institute Press, Washington, D.C.

CHAPTER 3

The Egyptians Barbara Watterson 1997 Balckwell Publishers Cambridge, Massachusetts

The Cambridge History of Africa Volume I: From the Earliest Times to 500b.c. J. Desmond Clark, ed. 1982 Cambridge University Press, Cambridge

African History Philip Curtin, Steven Feierman, Leonard Thompson and Jon Vansine 1978 Little, Brown and Co., London

The Ancient Egypt Site: The History of Ancient Egypt www.geocities.com/~amenhotep/history/main.html

The Decline of Empires S.N. Eisenstadt, ed. 1967 Prentice-Hall, Inc. Englewood Cliffs, N.J.

Citizenship Paul Barry Clarke 1994 Pluto Press, London

The European Inheritance: Volume I Sir Ernest Barker, Sir George Clark and Professor P. Vaucher, eds. 1954 Oxford University Press, London

An Ancient Economic History: From the Paleolithic Age to the Migrations of the Germanic, Slavic, And Arabic Nations Volume III
Fritz M. Heichelheim 1970 A.W. Sijthoff, Leyden, The Netherlands

From Alexander to Constantine: Passages and Documents Illustrating The History of Social and Political Ideas 336 B.C.-A.D. 337 Translated with Introductions, Notes and Essays by Ernest Barker 1956 Oxford University Press, London

Classics Ireland Volume III: Slavery in the Roman Empire Numbers and Origins
John Madden 1996 University College, Dublin, Ireland

The Social Contract and Discourse on the Origin of Inequality Jean-Jacques Rousseau 1967 Edited with an Introduction by Lester G. Crocker Simon & Schuster, Inc. New York, New York

The Portable Gibbon: The Decline and Fall of the Roman Empire
Edward Gibbon 1952 The Viking Press New York, New York

A Concise Economic History of the World: From Paleolithic Times to the Present
Rondo Cameron 1989 Oxford University Press, Oxford

The Rise of the West: A History of the Human Community
William H. McNeill 1963 University of Chicago Press, Chicago, Illinois

The Concise Columbia Electronic Encyclopedia, Third Edition Rulers of the Roman Empire (including dates of reign) www.encyclopedia.com/articles/11112.html
1994 Columbia University Press, New York, New York

Lords of All the World Anthony Pagden 1995 Yale University Press, New Haven, Connecticut

Trade and Dominion: The European Oversea Empires in the Eighteenth Century
J.H. Parry 1971 Weidenfeld and Nicolson, London

Global Expansion: Britain and its Empire 1870-1914
Willie Thompson 1999 Pluto Press, London

Empire: The British Imperial Experience 1765 to the Present
Denis Judd 1996 BasicBooks, New York, New York

Did British Capitalism Breed Inequality?
Jeffrey G. Williamson 1985 Routledge, New York, New York

The Idea of Poverty: England In The Early Industrial Age
Gertrude Himmelfarb 1983 Alfred A. Knopf, New York, New York

Wealth and Inequality in Britain W.D. Rubinstein 1986 Faber & Faber, Ltd., London

The People and The British Economy 1830-1914:
Roderick Floud 1997 Oxford University Press, Oxford, England

Pedagogy of the Oppressed
Paulo Freire 1996 The Continuum Publishing Company, New York, New York

Reform Acts The Victorian Web http://landow.stg.brown.edu/victorian/history/hist2.html Glenn Everett 1987

2003 FBI - *Uniform Crime Report*

FBI - Crime in the United States 1999

"DC Infant Mortality Rate Lowest Ever DC -Infant Mortality Rate Lowest Ever, But Still Higher the National Rate" *Associated Press*, Oct 21, 2005, Washington, D.C.

Dr. William Bowen California Geographical Survey, Department of Geography, California State University, Northridge, CA *Washington, D.C. and Vicinity 1990* (Maps)

United States Census Bureau Various Documents

CDC, US Bureau of Justice, The Sentencing Project and the Corrections Compendium

Atomic Audit: The Costs and Consequences of U.S. Nuclear Policy Since 1940 Stephen I. Schwartz 1998 Brookings Institution Press, Washington D.C.

CHAPTER 4

Europe and the People Without History Eric R. Wolf 1982 University of California Press, Berkeley, CA

Imperialism and Its Contradictions V.G. Kiernan 1995 Routledge, Inc. New York, London

Andrew Rosenthal "No Ground Fighting Yet; Call to Arms by Hussein" *The New York Times* January 17th, 1991, p. 1

"The Balance of Power in the Air: Who Has What" *The New York Times* January 17th, 1991, p. 15

Maureen Dowd "Storm's Eye: Bush Decides To Go to War" *The New York Times* January 17th, 1991, p. 16

Thomas L. Friedman "Barrage of Iraqi Missiles on Israel Complicates U.S. Strategy in Gulf" *The New York Times* January 18th, 1991, p. 1

The New York Times January 19th, 1991, p. 1 (Entire Page)

Eric Schmitt "Computerized Accuracy: 'A Relief to See the Tomahawks Fly'" *The New York Times* January 19th, 1991, p. 6

"Censors Screen Pooled Reports" *The New York Times* January 19th, 1991, p. 6

Thomas C. Hayes "Pride of a Texas Plant: The Fast and Agile F-16" *The New York Times* January 19th, 1991 p. 37-38

Patrick E. Tyler "U.S. War Plan: Still the Ground to Conquer" *The New York Times* January 20th, 1991, p. 1

"No Sign of Terrorism, But F.B.I. Is Preparing" *The New York Times* January 20th, 1991, p. 1

Joel Brinkley "Israel Says It Must Strike at Iraqis But Indicates Willingness to Wait"
The New York Times January 20th, 1991, p. 1

David E. Rosenbaum "Press and U.S. Officials at Odds on News Curbs"
The New York Times January 20th, 1991, p. 16

James Barron "Iraqi TV Broadcasts Interviews With 7 Identified as Allied Pilots"
The New York Times January 21st, 1991, p. 1

Thomas L. Friedman "Hard Times, Better Allies" *The New York Times* January 21st, 1991, p. 1

Malcolm W. Browne "Conflicting Censorship Upsets Many Journalists"
The New York Times January 21st, 1991, p. 10

Atomic Audit: The Costs and Consequences of U.S. Nuclear Policy Since 1940
Stephen I. Schwartz 1998 Brookings Institution Press, Washington D.C.

CHAPTER 5

A Garlic Testament: Seasons on a Small New Mexico Farm
Stanley Crawford 1998 University of New Mexico, Albuquerque, New Mexico

The War Business: Squeezing a Profit from the Wreckage in Iraq
Chalmers Johnson *Harper's Magazine*, November, 2003

Making a Killing: The Business of War 2002 The Center for Public Integrity

The Lexus and the Olive Tree Thomas Friedman 2000 Anchor Books, New York, New York

The World Development Report 2002 2003 The World Bank, Washington, D.C.

www.wri.org/wri/wr-96-97/ei_txt4.html World Resources Institute

Getting Ahead: Economic and Social Mobility in America Daniel P. McMurrer & Isabel V.
Sawhill, eds. 1998 The Urban Institute Press, Washington, D.C.

The Scorecard on Globalization 1980-2000: Twenty Years of Diminished Progress
Mark Weisbrot, Dean Baker, Egor Kraev and Judy Chen
(http://www.attac.org/fra/toil/doc/cepr05.htm)

ENDNOTES

CHAPTER 1

[i] Then, as now, whenever the words "freedom" or "democracy" are used by the ruling class to support a cause, one can generally substitute the words "power" or "money."

[ii] Jefferson's declaration, lofty in ambition that, "..all men are created equal," deserves, without any practical relevance, to be taken from the sacred canon and placed in the category of historical niceties, where, as a work of rhetorical fantasy, it belongs.

[iii] The condition of the poor fighting for the rich, like the subjugation of civil rights, also became a habit of American warfare, and is a trait of all empires.

[iv] He would get his wish: the original Senate was not directly elected by the people and was given a term three times the length of the popularly elected House.

CHAPTER 2

[i] It is better, for the sake of propriety, to refer to these elected officials as politicians, as the overwhelming majority are from one of the two monolithic political parties.

[ii] According to U.S. Census Bureau data, post WWII (roughly coinciding with the creation of the CIA in 1947) income inequality figures in the U.S. have been basically stagnant until the 1970's, and have become worse from that decade through the late 1990's. In addition, the poverty rate (in the neighborhood of 10-15% of the population) over the past three decades has remained unchanged. We must also remember that these poverty rates are actually on the very low end of the scale as the government's method for determining poverty does not include cost of living considerations.

[iii] While in reality the government of the Soviet Union was a one-party monopoly similar to the United States two-party oligarchy, the myth - because this particular monopoly explicitly managed state corporations - that it was a massive leftist conglomerate, helped to polarize the political debate in America. The Cold War was actuality a power struggle between two empires-justified through political propaganda-and was not based on ideology.

[iv] Although they were different parties, there were still only two.

[v] Targeting impoverished, powerless individuals is the preferred method because they have limited means to retaliate.

[vi] One need only throw a fleeting glance to the red scares during this period to witness the solidity of American freedom and democracy.

CHAPTER 3

[i] To qualify as an empire a state need not have a dictator, sultan, etc. at the top of the hierarchy, it needs only a dominant (few) and lesser (many) configuration: either dictatorships or ruling elite models fit the requirement.

[ii] The reason the latter case commonly occurs, lay in equal measure with a state revenging the suffering posited upon it by its previous master as it does to the close proximity of its master from which it gains the knowledge of how to wreak havoc, like a student from a teacher.

[iii] Coincidentally, this lesson has been implicitly ingested by the American imperialists, so well in fact that the former mother country has become a surrogate.

[iv] Although this is not an economic treatise, one would have to imagine that other factors beside the illegality of slavery contributed to the fall in Jamaica's sugar production, because society in the West Indies (as in many other British colonial possessions) continued to resemble its former hierarchical structure, minus state-sponsored slavery. It would have been possible for instance, to pay someone a penny a year and have them qualify as a "free" person.

[v] There were countless other atrocities from China to Australia to the South Pacific, so many that it would take several volumes to provide adequate details.

[vi] "The generosity of the oppressors is nourished by an unjust order, which must be maintained in order to justify that generosity." (Freire 1996, p. 42)

[vii] Quality of life issues such as urban alienation, crime, inhumane living conditions, and unsafe factories marked other changes from agrarianism.

[viii] Not really surprising, given that the country is only a few decades removed from being an apartheid state.

[ix] It is important to keep in mind that these numbers are based on federally determined poverty rates that reflect nationwide averages which do not vary based on geography (U.S. Census Bureau). Cost of living indexes in the major cities are generally much higher than those in rural areas of the country, thus the real rate of poverty in D.C. is substantially greater than the official numbers indicate.

[x] That a state is needed to grant people freedom is, at best, a dubious notion.

[xi] A circumstance, considering historical rhetoric of 'no taxation without representation,' that would be laughable if the results were not so tragic.

[xiii] Once again this is not intended as an abnegation of valid western accomplishments.

CHAPTER 4

ⁱ In empires' conduct, many factors could be considered as contributing to dissolution. I have chosen to focus in these next two chapters on militarism and corporations, not in an effort to apply limits to the scope of American decadence, but to point to what I believe are the principal precipitators of wrongful behavior.

ⁱⁱ Residents in areas around the globe which suffer from acute poverty, like U.S. inner cities, are often under a daily threat of violence.

ⁱⁱⁱ This is a familiar pattern in American propaganda efforts, and is similar to encouraging people to follow and be concerned with the fluctuations in the stock market. The average American has a paltry sum committed, as opposed to those leading the crusade, i.e. the 1% of Americans who own 42.1% of all stocks (incl. those in mutual funds and retirement accounts) and 10% of Americans who own 78.7% of all stocks (incl. those in mutual funds and retirement accounts). Edward N. Wolff *"Recent Trends in Wealth Ownership 1983-1998"* April 2000 Jerome Levy Economics Institute

^{iv} Especially when one considers the class issues involved. Much of the manufacturing base and human fodder for wars is and has been drawn largely from the poor, with many of these people believing, often justifiably, that other than serving, there is no other way out of their impoverished state. Special consideration also goes to those who were drafted into the service against their will. Although conscientious objection, notably in our more recent military endeavors, was a fairly well-publicized option to the draft.

^v An argument could be made that the Civil War was a fight over control of the expanding American Empire.

^{vi} This pre-Spanish American war list could include everything from the Monroe Doctrine, to efforts in Asia, the Caribbean, Mexico (the Mexican American war), South and Central America.

^{vii} An additional interesting note, revolves around *The New York Times* promoting America as a bastion of democracy (see previous references to Eckholm's article on China). How could any "news" establishment unabashedly further the myth of American democracy while slavishly operating with so little resistance under what could only be described as police-state policies?

^{viii} Incidentally, there were roughly 12.3% (U.S. Census Bureau) Americans living in poverty in 2006. Given how the U.S. Census Bureau calculates poverty, the actual number of poor people in the U.S. is much higher than the official number would allow.

^{ix} These motives are alluded to in the aforementioned *Annual Report*, i.e. that, "...activities aimed at denying U.S. access to vital energy supplies and key strategic resources will serve to undermine the legitimacy of friendly governments, disrupt key regions and sea lanes, and threaten the safety and well-being of U.S. citizens at home and abroad." (www.dtic.mil/execsec/adr2000/chap1.html, p. 2)

^x This too is mentioned in the report, "...the United States will retain the capability to act unilaterally when necessary..." (www.dtic.mil/execsec/adr2000/chap1.html, p. 3).

CHAPTER 5

i   Needless to say, this dominance was not without severe consequences for the native populations: millions of people were enslaved, killed or otherwise tormented under the lash of European tyranny.

ii   All of which was made ethically acceptable by the fact that most non-white races were seen as sub-human.

iii   There have been exceptions to the ruling elite, large-scale capital model and those have taken place in smaller jurisdictions within capitalist countries or in socialist/communist countries. But even the latter for the most part either succumbed to the current order (see China), or mimicked the ruling elite model under the guise of socialism/communism, with their own governmental elite (see Soviet Union, Maoist China).

iv   This stance, while by no means given top priority, is, as we have seen in the previous chapter, admitted by the Pentagon. Perhaps the only variance from official policy here is the level of importance placed on this role and the false equation of freedom and globalization proffered by the authorities.

v   Another side note is the rapidly expanding privatization of the U.S. military, which helps to illuminate any illusion of separation between the two entities. See *Making a Killing: The Business of War*, 2002, The Center for Public Integrity

vi   Although in some European circles, political parties exist which question the hegemony, their effect on the prevalent political direction of their countries remains limited.

vii   Once again, see the doctrines of the world's religious faiths for further information on this subject.

viii   Interesting to note is the government having the godlike power to bestow life.

ix   A little unexpected, compassionate boost, considering conventional arguments of the market's supposed amorality.

x   Of course conglomerates do posses the acumen to recognize when they need to move from unionized countries with expensive labor to countries lacking these things, but this does not demonstrate true adaptability, because their ideology remains constant.

xi   It needs to be re-emphasized that the question of morality regarding globalization has to do with the violence and suffering inherent to the model, rather than immorality stemming from simply stockpiling wealth. While it could be seen as objectionable to some if, for example, everyone on the planet were wealthy, but a few were wealthier than the majority, it would not, under this definition, necessarily be immoral.

CHAPTER 6

 i This governance format creates a breeding ground for gaping iniquity in the citizenry's wealth and standard of living.

ii It must be noted that the threat of violence, be it state or otherwise, is more challenging to quantify.

iii As the country's population has expanded, the number of voters per representative has increased exponentially.

iv The reference here is not to the thousands of small or mid-sized companies (although they often model the behavior found in their larger relatives), it is to multinational corporations.

v It would be hard to imagine, for example, a worker controlled and owned factory shutting themselves down so that they could make more money by exploiting foreign workers.

vi It should go without saying that the American court system historically and presently supports the ruling class more than any other, and that this support helps to legitimize (through corporate law, the incarceration of political prisoners, upholding draconian drug laws, promoting the death penalty, etc.) any number of egregious violations upon human dignity.

vii Countless examples of this type of adjustment have occurred throughout U.S. history. From drug laws designed to control the lower classes and minorities (i.e. crack cocaine carrying higher penalties than powder cocaine, three strikes legislation and mandatory sentencing for drug offenses), to wartime sedition legislation (from the first alien sedition act in 1798 to 2002's USA Patriot Act) which restrict dissent and civil liberties, the authorities are constantly searching for ways to use the law to erode whatever freedoms they can. These are laws that order brutal repression and a strangling conformity for their subjects.

viii Does not the word "public" imply some kind of equanimity, given the wealth of the country? Equanimity does not exist in the sphere of education because it is not a characteristic of imperial societies. One would expect, with a society based on the fundamentally flawed historical antecedents of empire, that its education system would be diseased.

ix "Public" radio and television in the United States are anything but. As time goes by, they have progressively relied more upon corporations and this has effected what limited independence they may once have had. For PBS, see William Hoynes *"The Cost of Survival: Political Discourse and the New PBS"*, 1999, www.fair.org/reports/pbs-study-1999.html and for NPR see www.fair.org/media-outlets/npr.html

x Voter turnout in the U.S. is so low that one can hardly say that these are true representatives.

xi This is not an argument regarding basic human needs, like sufficient food, water, shelter, leisure time, etc., it is an argument based on the cult of wasteful consumption.

xii Attacks against property, like military installations and weaponry, the storefronts of multinational corporations, etc., rather than against people, presents a more difficult problem, and are less of a clear cut moral issue.

xiii Although it does cause them some discomfort, and forces them to change their agendas. Two examples are lip service to the poor by organizations like the World Economic Forum and having to change their meeting places to remote, heavily guarded locations to keep clear of protesters.

xiv There are alternative ways to invest money. These usually involve community-based credit unions, which tend to be more cooperative and less exploitive, and generally keep their funds in the immediate locale.

xv This should not be viewed as approbation for the liberally inspired "green" living, investing, and eating movement. An individual cannot simply change what they buy -i.e. build an energy efficient mansion with sustainably harvested, local wood- and not make any other substantial changes to their lives, and view this as resistance or activism: it is neither.

xvi The description of home does not necessarily denote a single-family private residence; it could take many forms. There are also multitudes who are rootless, and desire to remain that way, so this might not be as relevant for them.

xvii For anyone spending time in or traveling through America, a truth that becomes quickly apparent is the number of eccentrics who populate the country. This is a strength of the people and is not attributable to state power, patriotism, or anything of that sort. When the time comes for the Empire's exit, this spirit of individuality and freakiness should help to make the coming era more enlightened.

.

www.ingramcontent.com/pod-product-compliance
Lightning Source LLC
Chambersburg PA
CBHW030249030426
42336CB00009B/317